HOW TO SCREW THE IRS

HOW TO SCREW THE IRS

First Edition

January, 1996

C. Richard Dobbins, Sr., CPA

Rustic Inn Publications, Inc.

Cover design by Paul York; 3533 Bishops Gate; Memphis, Tennessee 38115; Telephone 1-901-365-4418.

Printing by Fundco Printers; 407 Arendall Street; Adamsville, Tennessee 38310; Telephone 1-800-426-9827.

Library of Congress Cataloging-in-Publication Data

Dobbins, Sr., C. Richard

How to Screw the IRS / C. Richard Dobbins, Sr. —-First ed. paperback

Includes index.

ISBN 0-9650251-0-1

Library of Congress Catalog Card Number: 96-92020

Printed in the United States of America

To my family

About the Author

C. RICHARD DOBBINS, SR. is a practicing Certified Public Accountant in the accounting firm of Dobbins & Brawner, CPAs. Richard worked for one of the Big Six CPA firms in Memphis, Tennessee, for several years and was Secretary-Treasurer of a finance company chain before returning to his hometown to begin his CPA practice. Richard and his wife, Peggy, live on a small farm in Corinth, Mississippi. Richard and Peggy have two sons and a daughter. All three children are accountants.

Contents

Preface

For most, reading about taxes and tax planning is not one of our favorite endeavors. Many books are too technical and do not attempt to give the reader a practical approach to tax planning and tax savings.

I have been talking about writing this book for 15 to 20 years with hopes that it will give the reader some help, courage, and confidence when he has any type of encounter with the IRS and will also give some practical hints that have been helpful to me in dealing with the IRS and other taxing agents over the years. I am appreciative that another author, Craig Ryan from Portland, Oregon, gave me the encouragement to begin the book.

I would also like to give special thanks to Mrs. Ruth Sharp, my high school English teacher, and Mrs. Marcia Oden, from Jackson, Mississippi for the help they provided in proofing this book. Also, a big thanks to Mrs. Paulette Rogers, for her help in reviewing the technical portion of the book. I also thank the IRS agents that furnished information and data.

I wish each reader less taxing experiences with the IRS, and hope that you are very successful in your business endeavors.

C. Richard Dobbins, Sr.

Chapter 1

Introduction

EACH PAYDAY WHETHER WE ARE A BLUE collar worker in Mississippi or a New York banker, we are reminded that the tax man comes and takes away up to fifty percent or more of our paychecks. We each ask how we can increase our paychecks and decrease these taxes that continue to take such a toll on our hard-earned pay.

Because of the increased tax burden, most taxpayers continue to attempt to find ways to reduce their taxes either through legal tax planning or by other methods.

I will explore in this book some tax planning techniques that will save each of us some of our hard-earned pay by reducing our tax burden as well as giving us the satisfaction and some knowledge of "How to Screw the IRS."

I have attempted to produce a non-technical book that is easy to understand. I have tried to keep the text short and to the point so that the reader will enjoy reading about taxes and tax planning. In chapters eleven and twelve, because of the nature of the taxes and credits discussed, some technical information has been presented, but it should be easy to read and understand.

There are no known ways to provide unique and painless journeys through Revenue Rulings, the Internal Revenue Code and Regulations, Tax Court cases and other IRS rulings. Hopefully this book will give each reader the building blocks to become just a little more tax literate in dealing with all of these complex items that the IRS has forced on our daily lives.

The federal deficit or national debt is now running around 5 trillion dollars and increasing at an alarming rate each day. With this continued over spending that our congressmen are allowing to take place, we each should be concerned about the financial stability of our government. We should all also realize that when our government leaders are talking about tax cuts, but continue to allow spending to go on unchecked, we all eventually will have to pay more taxes to help balance the budget and pay the national debt.

In this book, I will discuss legal methods of doing tax planning to reduce our tax burden. I will also discuss methods used by some taxpayers to evade taxes. Tax planning and the related reduction in taxes are legal and are permitted by the IRS, while methods used to evade taxes are illegal and are vigorously pursued by the IRS. In some cases, the taxpayer convicted of tax evasion will serve time in federal prisons or will at least have to pay some very hefty taxes, interest, and penalties.

I encourage each one to do his tax planning legally and to pay any taxes that may be legally due and in no way would encourage anyone to evade taxes. The illegal methods of evading taxes discussed in this book should not be attempted by any reader. They will surely cause anyone trying to use any of them some very costly tax advisors to represent them before the IRS. They also present the possibility of having to pay large penalties to the IRS or the possibility of serving time in the federal prisons.

I also encourage you throughout the book to obtain professional tax advice. Because of the ever changing tax laws, and because of the complexity of the tax laws, this book should not be used as a substitute for professional tax advice.

Chapter 2

When the IRS Comes Knocking

WHEN MOST OF US RECEIVE ANY CORRESPONDENCE from the IRS, including our annual tax return filing forms, we feel intimidated. We wonder if we are the next unlucky ones who will be checked or harassed by these people who seem to have so much power over our every day life and our ability to make a living. I have even had some clients who have actually become sick and been checked into a hospital after receiving these much dreaded notices from the IRS.

The IRS can come knocking in many different ways. You may receive a letter from them notifying you that an agent or auditor will be reviewing a personal or business tax return, or they may request other documents that you are required to file with them on a continuing basis. However, since the improvement of the IRS computer system, most of us are now receiving reams of notices stating that we have not filed the appropriate form. Or they may have received a notice from a third party, such as a bank or other business that has issued a Form 1099, showing that some sum of money has been paid to us and that the IRS is unable to locate this amount on our tax return. As a result, the IRS instructs us that because of this oversight on our part we need to send them a certain amount of tax, penalties, and interest along with a copy of the notice, and then every thing will be okay.

Also, the IRS comes knocking when a collection agent comes to our home or business to ask about some tax that they think is due. Or they may ask about a current or past employee that they are trying to track down for one reason or another. Most of these collection agents can be very intimidating and can put pressure on you to answer any question they may have no matter how insignificant we may believe the question is.

The most dreaded visit by an IRS agent comes when an agent with the IRS Criminal Investigation Division (CID) shows up at our front door with badge in hand and begins asking questions about our tax dealings or the dealings of someone that we know. Usually one of the first things these agents tell you about is your miranda rights. This actually means that they are trying to develop information to put you or others in jail. Of all the agents that come knocking, the CID agent is the most dangerous; therefore, you must be very careful what you say to them.

No matter how the IRS comes knocking, there are tactics that one must remember and develop when dealing with them. More details of suggested tactics are listed in this chapter to help you know what move and counter move to consider once you have been contacted by them.

When the IRS Sends Notice of Additional Taxes Due

As previously mentioned, the IRS has become more proficient with their computer systems. Consequently we are all being inundated with more and more IRS notices about all kinds of taxes and forms that we have either not filed or that we have filed, and the IRS feels that the forms are incorrect. With the many such notices that I have dealt with over many years, I have found that probably 90% or more of these notices are incorrect, and in many cases no additional tax is due. Usually filing the form requested by the IRS is not required. Of the notices where tax is owed, generally only a small amount of the tax, penalty, and interest is actually due.

Many of these notices are for bank interest paid to taxpayers or dividends paid from various corporations. Often these notices are for Forms 1099 that businesses are required to mail each year. These show the amount of payments that they have made to you or your business. The errors that are found on the bank interest statements and the corporate dividend statements are usually from the incorrect names or social security numbers shown on these documents. Usually, you can correct these errors from the bank and other corporate entities by notifying the IRS that the income was not your income and that it has properly been recorded as taxable income on another tax return. If you can send a copy of the return on which the income was reported, then you should receive a quick reply from the IRS stating that they have accepted your information as submitted and that no additional tax or correspondence is needed. If they do not accept your explanation, they will usually notify you what else they want you to mail to them.

The notices from the IRS for the Forms 1099 income not being reported or under reported on your tax return are usually mailed to you if the IRS has trouble matching these third party forms to your individual tax return. These amounts can be reported on page 1 of Form 1040, on schedules C, D, E, F, 4835, 6252, and on other schedules and forms. There are so many places on your return for these amounts to be reported, there is no doubt that the IRS will miss many of these items when they are being cross checked by their computer system. When you receive these notices, and you know that you have in fact reported the correct amount, you need to write the IRS and tell them where the amount has been reported on your return. Mail the IRS a copy of the related form, circle the amount in question in red or some other color, and state the notation in your letter to the IRS.

Many of the notices are indeed completely in error; therefore, instead of being intimidated by receiving the notice from the IRS, we should probably be upset that the IRS makes so many errors in their notices. We as citizens and taxpayers should insist through our senators and congressmen that the IRS be more accountable and be required to either make a much better effort to send out correct notices or not send out notices at all.

Never, never mail the IRS the taxes requested on these forms just because you feel intimidated or afraid that they may question some other area on your return. Actually intimidation may give way to making you just plain angry about receiving such notices, and you will probably correspond more effectively with the IRS being mad rather than intimidated. Occasionally you may have to correspond with the IRS two to five times before you receive the notice that they finally have accepted your return as filed and that you owe no further tax in the matter that they have written you about. At times, it appears that the IRS finally accepts your data and gives up on their continued correspondence with you after you have written to them four or five times. It surely does make you feel good to take on the IRS and go from the feeling of being intimidated to one of pride from beating them at their own game of unnecessary correspondence.

Another important fact to remember when corresponding with the IRS is that after you have sent your original correspondence and you end up having to write another letter, you then can also send a copy of this second correspondence to the Problems Resolution Division of the IRS. These offices have some very astute agents that process and resolve problems that the regular service centers can either not resolve or will not take the time to resolve. Do not overlook this division of the IRS. You can even sometimes consider them somewhat friendly, especially after you have tried so hard to resolve the questions raised by the IRS directly with the agent or service center from which you originally received the notice.

At the end of this book are example letters that you may find useful in corresponding with the IRS initially or with the problems resolution division. You will be able to modify each letter to your individual correspondence needs.

When the IRS Sends a 100% Penalty Notice

When the IRS sends you a notice about a 100% penalty for unpaid payroll taxes, even though you may or may not own the business, you get a very big sinking feeling. You wonder how the IRS can want to collect the payroll taxes due, and then assess you and possibly several others the 100% penalty for the unpaid payroll taxes. For these past due payroll taxes, the IRS will "reach out and touch someone" until they are able to find someone connected to the business who either has cash or other assets and will pay this tax. This tax can usually be assessed to company owners, corporate officers, and employees that are responsible for withholding and depositing the payroll taxes. If you work for a company having cash flow problems, and you are responsible for preparing and signing the payroll checks, or making the payroll tax deposits, you should refuse to take this responsibility. The first time your employer does not make the payroll tax deposit on a timely basis, you should be alerted that you should quit signing payroll checks. Then let your employer know that he will need to sign all future payroll checks and tax deposit checks. Also, if you are an officer or director of the company, you should consider resigning, so that the IRS will have no reasons to assess you with this 100% payroll tax penalty. In this type of situation, the earlier that you can remove yourself from any type of payroll work, the less likelihood exists that the IRS will be able to assess you. If a collection agent does assess you for this 100% penalty, and you believe that you have no reason for being assessed, you should ask to meet with the collection agent's supervisor. If this does not resolve the assessment, you should ask to have the assessment sent to the Appeals Division of the IRS. When you meet with the Appeals Division, you should take your tax professional with you or let him attend the meeting by himself. When you do get one of these notices, you should not procrastinate; you should begin acting on the notice immediately, so that you can resolve the assessment as soon as possible. Of course, if you carry the assessment to the appeals division, it will probably take six to nine months before you receive your decision as to the assessment being abated.

When the IRS Sends a Notice to Audit Your Return

When you prepare taxes professionally, and you get a telephone call from a client who starts the conversation by saying that we have problems, you can usually guess correctly that the taxpayer has received a letter from the IRS stating that a certain tax return is going to be audited.

Usually, the IRS will give you a two to five week notice that your return has been picked for auditing. If you need additional time to prepare for the audit, a telephone call to the agent will usually get you an additional two to three weeks of preparation time.

There are many different types of audits that the IRS performs. The most simple audit is just checking one or two items on your return, such as contribution deductions and interest deductions. Probably the most complex audit that the IRS performs is the Taxpayer Compliance Measurement Program (TCMP) audit, where every item on your return is checked and verified by the agent. On this compliance audit the agent is helping develop data to provide the IRS with a Discriminant Income Function scoring system (DIF). This will be used to compare to all other tax returns filed and will give the IRS the probability that additional tax is owed on another return if the DIF score is relatively high. Since it takes so much taxpayer time and expense for a compliance audit to be performed by the IRS, congress is proposing to pass a sequel to the Taxpayer's Bill of Rights. This would reimburse $222 million in refundable tax credits to the unfortunate taxpayers that are selected for these TCMP audits. The additional time and expense required to prepare for such an audit, as well as the additional time for meeting with the agent while the compliance audit is being performed would be repaid to the taxpayer with these tax credits. Additional information is provided in Chapter 9 about the TCMP audits performed by the IRS.

The IRS may also audit your business payroll tax returns. This ascertains if you are maintaining all W-4 withholding forms and are withholding a sufficient amount of taxes from each employee's pay. It also checks whether you are then remitting the related taxes on a timely basis and are preparing all of the monthly, quarterly, and yearly payroll reports accurately and on time.

When you receive the IRS notice that one or two items will be audited on your tax return, you should immediately get your copy of your return along with all of the backup data that you have retained for the period to be audited. You should check to see that all documentation requested by the IRS is present in your data and that the data is accurate. If you find that any information being requested for audit has not been retained in your records, you should begin immediately to reconstruct the data. You may have to call your bank to request interest or dividend income statements or call your bank or mortgage company to request mortgage interest statements. You may need to contact your church treasurer to request contribution records for the period being audited. If you find any of your data that you originally included on your return to be inaccurate, you should review other items on your return to determine if there are any other inaccuracies. Then you can determine any major changes that you may be facing during the audit. Many times when an error that will cost you additional tax is made on your return, you can find other items that will reduce your tax in other areas of your return. If you have to spend so much time preparing for and attending your IRS audit, you should make every effort to find any additional items that may reduce your tax on the return being audited. If you want to shift attention away from a particular item being audited, merely show the agent one or two items that you have found that will reduce your taxes. Many times this will shift the audit away from a weak position that you may have on your return to an area that will assure that you will receive a refund from this IRS audit. Also, a very positive point to remember is that if the IRS audits particular areas of your return and does not find anything that yields additional tax, then the IRS is not supposed to audit these particular items for the next two years. It has been considered to be taxpayer harassment if the IRS continues to ask to audit the same items year after year without any additional tax being assessed.

If you represent yourself at the IRS exam, you should volunteer only two words during the examination, and those are "Hello" and "Good-bye". After you greet the agent, you should not make small talk or attempt to impress the agent with your vast knowledge of anything, but just answer the agent's questions with as little discussion and with as few words as possible. Never volunteer anything and make the agent ask about anything that he may want to know. If you do not know how to answer a question that the agent is asking, you should not try to make up an answer. Tell the agent that you will have to get back with him with the answer. If at anytime during your audit, you feel that you are being pressured or are being treated rudely, be sure to ask the agent to let you speak with his immediate supervisor. These intimidating tactics used by some agents will usually change immediately.

Probably the best money that you will ever spend is to hire a tax professional to either represent you at your audit or to accompany you to the audit meeting. I, as well as many other tax professionals, will tell the tax client that unless the IRS agent specifically requests the taxpayer or taxpayers to be present, then the tax professional will attend the audit session by himself and will not have the taxpayer present. Many times the agent will not know this in advance, and his reaction will vary when he finds out that the tax professional is present without the taxpayer. Often times the tax professional goes to the IRS office to meet with a new agent with whom he has never worked, and the agent comes out at the appointed time and asks if the representative is the taxpayer. When the tax professional identifies himself and relates that he has the taxpayer's power-of-attorney and will be representing the taxpayer, it is often the agent who actually gets nervous. Knowing that the agent was hoping to make the taxpayer nervous, and then putting the shoe on the other foot, certainly makes you feel good as the tax professional.

Also, in audits such as this, the tax professional can usually help control the direction of the audit and can usually guide the agent to areas that have good support and away from areas that have weak support. Your tax professional should also be able to help you find other areas on your return that may get you a refund rather than make you owe additional taxes. If the agent asks your tax professional a question that does not need to be answered or cannot be answered without implicating your owing many additional tax dollars, your representative can usually tell the agent that he will get back to him with the answer. Many times the agent will let the question go unanswered because of time constraints placed on them by their audit supervisors. Be sure to remember that if you do attend the audit with your tax professional, let him do the talking and you answer only the questions that he directs you to answer.

If you do decide to represent yourself during the audit, and it appears that the audit is not going well for you, you should tell the agent that you want to terminate the current audit session, and that you want to reschedule so that you can bring your tax professional with you. Many times this will upset the agent. But who cares; let him be upset. Just do whatever you have to do so that you do not end up paying a lot of extra taxes that you may not have to pay.

If you do represent yourself and you believe that the agent's final decisions and adjustments are not correct, you should ask the agent for a meeting with his supervisor. If you still think that you have not gotten a fair deal, tell the supervisor that you want to meet with an IRS appeals agent. You may have to file an appeals document to be able to meet with this appeals agent; however, you can request a sample appeals document from the supervisor, and you can usually just fill in the blanks. Many of these appeals agents will give in to many of the items questioned just to be able to resolve the appeal at this level to keep the appeal process from going to the next level of tax court. If you do go to the appeals level by yourself, and without representation, be sure to be prepared for a good presentation of your data and documentation. Be able to refer the appeals agent to IRS publications and other IRS documents and literature when arguing your various points.

Never agree to an audit assessment amount during the audit, but tell the agent that you will review the assessment items and will let him know if you agree or disagree with the assessment amount.

Also, if you are being represented by a tax professional, never agree to meet with the agent by yourself. Many of the agents are requesting to come by the taxpayer's house or business to ask a few questions or get some additional information. In some instances, the agent has just shown up at the front door of the taxpayer's house or business without calling. He states that he needs to ask some questions or get additional information. You should advise the agent that you have a tax representative as permitted under the Taxpayer Bill of Rights and that you will not meet with the agent nor discuss anything with the agent without your representative present. If the agent appears to be upset because of your refusal to meet with him without your representative present, so be it. If you refuse to let the agent into your house or business or refuse to talk with the agent over the telephone the first time he comes by or calls, he will probably not make anymore "burnt" runs or needless telephone calls to your home or business. If you do ever agree to meet with one of these agents by yourself, and without your tax professional present, the agent will usually continue to pressure you to meet with him without your tax professional present. Do not let this happen.

When meeting with the agent, be courteous but firm. Do not show your temper or your emotions, and under no circumstances make any verbal or any other type of threat to the agent. Be sure not to engage the agent in conversation, and do not let the agent engage you in idle conversation. You might consider taking your favorite magazine with you so that you will not be tempted to talk with the agent.

Chapter 3

Legal Tax Saving Techniques

REGARDLESS OF OUR AGE OR STATION IN life, each one of us strives continually to find the ultimate tax saving techniques, and we want to find the way to screw the IRS legally. When our day does finally come to be visited by an IRS agent, we want to be able to tell him that our tax planning techniques have been so unique and so perfect that we just dare him to find something wrong with our return.

After having this thought, we are suddenly reminded that this is the real world and that some of the things that we would like to tell the IRS agent must only be thought, not even whispered, and certainly not be told to our visiting IRS agent. With this in mind, we must then set out to develop some very sound tax saving ideals and techniques for our individual income bracket and our individual business endeavors.

In planning our tax saving techniques, many things must be taken into consideration. These include our salaries or earnings for each year, whether our employer has a pension or profit sharing plan, and if we will be able to itemize our deductions on our return. We must consider our marital status and if we will be willing or financially able to use some of our salary or earnings to spend or invest in tax saving plans or tax shelters.

One must remember there are many tax saving plans or tax shelters that can be used to reduce our tax burden each year; however, you must be willing to spend some of your earnings or money to invest in these plans and shelters to access this reduced tax burden.

Some of the tax saving plans and tax shelters that I will discuss in this chapter are IRAs, SEPs, SARSEPs, 401K plans, pension and profit sharing plans, cafeteria plans, and tax sheltered annuities. Only 25% of retirees have social security as their primary source of retirement income. The majority of retirees list the primary source of their retirement income as being these plans. These plans are very important for tax savings now and for your secured retirement later.

I will also discuss some considerations about starting a business venture to help shelter some of our earnings. And I will examine whether the business should be a sole-ownership, a partnership, or some type of corporation. Some of the business areas that will be covered will be farming, selling, and service type businesses.

Individual Retirement Accounts (IRAs)

Most of us have heard of this very simple tax shelter called an IRA; however, it seems that even though IRAs have been around for years, many taxpayers have not used this as a tax shelter for one reason or another. I find that many taxpayers will not set up an IRA because of the paperwork sent to us by the different banks, life insurance companies, and brokerage firms. We are overwhelmed by the pages and pages of legal and technical language that often accompany these mailings. IRAs are really simple and are very easy to understand, once you know the simple facts about them and leave the complex legal jargon alone. Your banker, your charter life underwriter (CLU), your broker, or your CPA should be able to tell you in five minutes or less about an IRA and whether it will be beneficial to you in your yearly tax planning quest for lower taxes and a more financially secure future.

I suggest that if you are 30 years old or older, you and your spouse should put the maximum amount in your IRA account each year if you are not covered by other types of plans at your place of employment. Some tax professionals recommend that these amounts be placed in your IRA accounts each year whether or not they are deductible on your tax return. However, I do not suggest making non-deductible contributions because it is difficult to keep up with the deductible and non-deductible portion of your plans until you start withdrawing the funds at the time of your retirement.

Remember that these funds will not be drawn out for retirement purposes for many years. Be sure that you place your IRA funds and other retirement funds in a bank, life insurance company, or brokerage firm that you believe has strong financial assets for the long term commitment required for these funds.

Many taxpayers are able to set up roll-over IRA accounts when they receive distributions from qualified pension and profit sharing plans or from 401K plans. The taxpayer has 60 days to roll these funds over to an IRA account to keep from having to pay taxes on them, and in most cases, a 10% early distribution penalty to the IRS. Some of the qualified plans have common stock held in the plans, and upon distribution the stock is distributed to the taxpayer creating a taxable distribution. If you receive such a distribution, you can usually set up a self-directed IRA account and roll these common stock shares over to avoid paying taxes on this distribution. Your broker or CLU can usually help you set up these self directed IRA accounts.

Simplified Employee Pension (SEPs)

These simplified employee pension plans are also referred to as SEPIRAs, and the employer makes contributions to different SEPIRA accounts for each employee who can participate in the plan. These plans are usually found in businesses where there are no employees or very few employees. Currently the maximum amount that can be placed in this plan by an owner-employee is $22,500. These plans require very little documentation to set up and do not require any filing of annual returns with the IRS. Usually, your bank, CLU, or broker can help you set up these accounts for yourself as well as for your employees. Since any covered employee makes the decision where their contributed funds will be placed, the company and the owners do not take on any fiduciary responsibilities as with other type plans. These plans normally allow the company to contribute up to 15% of your salary or self employed earnings to the plan each year on earnings up to $150,000. The contribution is deductible by the company and is not included in the employee's W-2.

The few negative things about these plans do not usually keep a company from setting them up. The negative things include the fact that all employees 21 years of age and over are covered by the plan, even if they work part time. Also, another negative is that the employee is fully vested in the plan contributions immediately upon the contribution being made to the plan. If an employee decides to leave the company the day after the contribution is made, or if he decides that he wants to withdraw the funds immediately, then the employee may do so.

The three types of SEP plans are the self-directed, mutual funds, and SEPs provided through insurance companies. The self-directed plan permits you to direct your funds to be invested in stocks, bonds, certificates of deposits, and other selected investments. The mutual fund SEP allows you to place your funds into many different types of investments. The mutual fund investments are good to use for the employees who know very little about stocks and bonds and investing. The SEPs provided through insurance companies permit you to place your funds into many different investments.

I suggest that any owner-employee who is the only person in a sole-owner business take full advantage of this plan and make the maximum contribution to his plan each year. If you have one or more employees who are not highly compensated, these plans can still be very useful in helping the self-employed person to place relatively large contributions in his plan each year. While annual contributions can be made to these SEPIRA accounts, you are not required to make them each year. Therefore, if your company experiences a year with little profit and tight cash-flow, the employer can make the decision not to contribute to the plan during the current year.

Salary Reduction Simplified Employee Pension (SARSEPs)

These plans are similar to the SEP plans, except that the employees place a portion of their salary in these plans through salary reductions. The portion of the salary reduction that is placed in these plans is not subject to federal or state income taxes, but it is subject to social security and medicare taxes. By the employees' contributing a portion of their salaries to the plan, the amount contributed by the employer is generally reduced. In many of these plans, the employees will contribute 6% of their salary and the employer will match the contribution with 6%. The maximum amount that an employee can defer into these SARSEP plans is 15%, but it is limited by an annual indexed amount. The annual indexed amount for 1995 was $9,240. The maximum amount that can be contributed to both the SEP and the SARSEP for the year is the lesser of 15% of compensation or $30,000. More employers with 25 or fewer eligible employees are beginning to use these plans. The eligible employees include the business owners, and at least 50% of eligible employees must participate in the plan. These plans closely resemble 401K plans; however, these plans do not have the costly reporting and administration fees associated with 401K plans.

I suggest that you participate in this plan for the maximum amount so that you can obtain the tax savings now and have more retirement income later.

401K Plans

The 410K plan has become the plan of choice of many employers with more than 25 employees. They choose it because the employee is required to contribute to the plan through salary reduction, thereby reducing the amount of the plan contributions by the employer. As previously mentioned, these plans work very much as do the SARSEPs; however, some part-time employees are not covered by the plan, and there is a vesting period for the employer's contribution to the plan. The annual information returns required by the IRS and the annual testing and administration of these plans are usually very expensive. When setting up one of these plans, you should ask the plan administrator to give you an estimation of cost for the coming 5 to 7 year period so that you will not be floored the first time you receive an annual administration fee of $4,000 to $5,000.

I suggest that you take full advantage of your employer's 401K plan and defer the maximum allowed amount of your salary.

In December 1995, the IRS and other government agencies were investigating approximately 300 companies for abuse of their 401K plans. Some of these companies are using the employee's funds for financing the company operations. Or they may divert the funds for the benefits of the company owners or officers. When signing up to participate in your company's plan, be sure to ask where your funds are being invested and ask fellow employees how the plan has performed in the past several years. Also, be sure that you receive annual plan reports that show your contributions, the employer contributions, and the earnings.

You should always feel comfortable with the investments that the plan administrators are making. Do not hesitate to roll your funds out of your 401K plan and into an IRA roll over account if you believe that your funds are not being managed and invested wisely.

Qualified Pension and Profit Sharing Plans

Many of the larger employers have qualified pension and profit sharing plans that can range from the simple Keogh plans (HR 10) to the more complex plans that are tailored to the individual employer's business or needs. The more complex plans have to be approved by the IRS, while the simpler Keogh plans usually have a prototype plan that the IRS has pre-approved and can usually be adopted by the employer with very little effort. The simple Keogh plans, as well as the more complex plans, can usually be set up through your CLU, your broker, or through your bank. Since all of these plans require annual filings of information returns with the IRS, you should be sure to ask the company administrating your plan if the fees you are paying for the administration covers all filling costs and administration fees. These plans have to be amended on a recurring basis to comply with the IRS and other governmental agencies ever changing rules and regulations. Therefore, you should also find out from your administrator how much you will be expected to pay each time the plans are revised. Also, most of these plans require that you pay a fee to the IRS each time they are revised. Many of these plans allow for employee contributions but do not require it, and very seldom does the employee contribute to these plans.

Cafeteria Plans

Many of the larger employers are providing cafeteria plans for their employees. This lets medical and other items such as child care be paid with the employee's before tax dollars, rather than after tax dollars.

Medical expenses and medical insurance are not generally deductible by the taxpayer on the itemized deduction Schedule A because of the large 7 1/2% exemption that must be met before deducting any medical expenses. These cafeteria plans are very beneficial to the employee since they can pay for their medical insurance, medical bills, eye exams and glasses, and child care expenses.

The employee decides the amount of salary reduction that he will put into the cafeteria plan, and then these funds are used to pay the related covered expenses. These funds are placed in the cafeteria plan before any tax deduction. So none of these funds are subject to federal withholding, state withholding, social security, or medicare taxes. Because of the exemption from social security and medicare taxes, the employer will also save these taxes on these funds. Other savings that the employer will have from these plans come from the federal unemployment taxes, state unemployment taxes, and reduction on workmen compensation insurance. This results from the reduction of the salary to these employees for the amount of the funds placed in the cafeteria plan.

Of course any time there is a savings from all of the taxes and workman compensation insurance, there must be some negative item. Otherwise all employers would set up one of these plans. The reason that most small employers do not set up these plans is that it takes time and expense to administer. The administrator must keep up with all plan expenditures of each participant. This means that each time an expenditure is made the plan administrator must be presented with a paid bill for reimbursement purposes. Getting everyone to supply these paid bills is usually very difficult and in some cases impossible.

If your company is approached about using an outside third party administrator to administer your cafeteria plan, be sure to ask if all required forms will be filed by this third party administrator and get a projection of administration costs for the next three to five years. Many of these third party administrators will try to sell your employees life insurance or disability insurance for the amount of taxes that the employee will be saving by using this plan. The selling of this life and disability insurance is another way for these third party administrators to make additional income from administrating these plans. However, the employees generally do not have enough life and disability insurance, and this is a very cost effective way to help provide this coverage with no reduction in net spendable income.

Tax Sheltered Annuities (TSAs)

There are two types of tax sheltered or tax deferred annuities. One is acquired with before tax dollars, and the other is acquired with after tax dollars. The first is fully taxable to you as you withdraw the funds. The one acquired with after tax dollars is taxable to you for only the amount of tax free earnings that have accumulated. You are taxed in proportion to your withdrawal amount. Therefore, if 10% of the funds are from tax free earnings, then 10% of your withdrawal would be taxed to you upon withdrawal.

The tax sheltered annuity that is acquired with before tax dollars is usually offered by schools, universities, and other governmental agencies. Most of these employers already have other types of retirement plans for their employees and also offer these TSAs on a voluntary basis to their employees so that additional funds can be saved with before tax dollars. If you work for an employer that offers such a plan, you should consider placing as much as you can into these plans.

Many banks, life insurance companies, and brokerage firms offer the tax deferred annuity acquired with after tax dollars. You can usually acquire these tax deferred annuities with a varying number of years and with many pay out options for yourself and your beneficiaries. Since these are usually set up for tax free accumulation of earnings for long term growth, be sure that you are financially able to set these funds aside for this type of investment.

There are many different types of other annuities with different pay out options that you should explore with your tax professional when you have extra funds to invest.

Other Tax Shelters

Each of us wants to know all of the tax shelters that the rich and famous use to reduce their taxes each year. We all have heard of the real estate limited partnerships that were supposed to save you thousands of dollars of taxes each year. We have also heard that to save many dollars in taxes each year, we should purchase different types of rental real estate.

Ten to fifteen years ago, there were all kinds of real estate limited partnerships that promised you many deductions and investment tax credits that could be used on your personal or corporate tax returns each year. Many taxpayers bought into these limited partnerships, and the tax laws changed almost immediately. Not only did these taxpayers not get to take many of the deductions, but they also found that they had a long term obligation to make payments on these investments with little or no deduction allowed on their returns. Many taxpayers tried to sell their investments in these limited partnerships, but they found that there was no market since the deductions had been eliminated or limited. Many of these real estate limited partnerships have gone broke, and this has permitted the taxpayer to at least take a deduction on their returns for the investments that they made for these tax shelters.

About the only tax shelter that the tax laws have not completely eliminated is the low-income housing investments. With these investments, the taxpayer usually does not have a limitation as to the deduction and credit amounts. Of course, with other types of passive loss deductions, the taxpayer may not be able to take any of the loss deduction, but he merely carries the passive loss forward each year until the investment is sold. Then he adds this unused passive loss carryover to the basis of the investment to figure the gain or loss.

When investing in one of these low-income housing limited partnerships, be sure to review all of the data with your tax professional to help assure yourself that the investment is not going to have deduction limitations on your tax return. Another important thing to remember is that the tax laws could also change again and eliminate any further deductions on these low-income housing limited partnerships.

Many taxpayers believe that by investing in any type of

rental real estate they will be able to save taxes due to the depreciation and other deductions. Prior to March 16, 1984, the tax laws permitted real estate to be depreciated over a 15 year period under the accelerated cost recovery system. Then the real estate depreciation years were increased to 18 years from March 16, 1984, to May 8, 1985. Again, the tax laws were changed increasing the depreciation years to 19 years from May 9, 1985, to December 31, 1986. As of January 1, 1987, the residential rental property depreciation life increased to 27 1/2 years, and the nonresidential rental property depreciation life increased to 31 1/2 years. As of May 13, 1993, the nonresidential rental property life was increased to 39 years. Since the depreciation life has more than doubled since 1984, the tax deduction for the related depreciation has decreased. This makes investments in rental real property and the purchase of a commercial building for your business less desirable. In making a decision today as to whether to lease or buy a commercial building for your business, you are probably going to have more deductions for lease expense than for depreciation expense.

One of the bigger decisions to be made in deciding to lease or buy is whether or not you want to have a business building in which you are building an equity interest.

Your decision to buy rental real estate will not then be made so much from the tax deduction received, but from the economic and investment advantages you will receive. Many taxpayers that invest regularly in rental real estate expect their investments to pay for themselves in 7 to 10 years and look for their real estate investments to help them hedge against inflation. Most values of real estate have increased faster than inflation, except in a few parts of the country. And after real estate prices become depressed in some areas, they usually increase in value within a few years. With building material prices increasing at a high rate, we will probably see rental real estate prices continue to increase at a price much in excess of inflation.

Some investors are using the technique of buying and paying for these rental real estate investments while they have a job or business, and then they use the rental income to supplement their social security benefits upon retirement. This rental income, unlike earned income, does not decrease the amount of social security benefits that the person can draw. If you have 10 to 15 residential rental houses paid for at age 62, you may be able to retire at an early age and from rental income have a good cash flow that will not decrease your monthly social security check.

Another planning technique used with residential rental property is to keep the property until it appears that repairs are becoming more than routine. Then sell the property and finance part of the selling price. The interest received is usually more than the amount that is being paid by your bank, and the interest and the long term gain being reported on the sale does not affect the amount of the social security benefits that you receive since these amounts are considered unearned income.

Can a Business Help Shelter Some of My Income?

We often hear that all types of business people are able to shelter much of their income by having tax loop holes that are not available to employees whose salaries are included on a W-2. This may seem to be unfair to the middle income taxpayer who generally receives a W-2 for his earnings. Most people who do have businesses that are required to file a business Schedule C, a farm Schedule F, a partnership return, or a corporate income tax return will usually pay less on their gross earnings than the W-2 earner. This is because of the deductions that can be taken on these business returns. Of course, all of us realize that some of the deductions may be questionable deductions. But with the IRS checking only a small percentage of returns, most of the businesses that take these questionable deductions will never be audited, so all of the deductions will go unnoticed by the IRS. If the IRS does decide to audit one of these companies and finds that there are some deductions that should not be taken, then only three year's of the questionable deductions will be changed, as the statute of limitation will have run on the other years.

Many of the businesses today can be classified into just a few categories such as farming, selling, and service businesses. Each of these categories has many sub-categories. For example, farming may be row crops, tree farming, cattle, horses, pond raised fish; the list goes on and on. The same is true for the selling and the service businesses, and these two categories will have many more sub-categories than farming.

After deciding which business venture to begin, then the decision must be made as to which type of business structure to use in running this business. Should you select a sole-ownership, a partnership, a limited liability partnership, a regular corporation or a sub-chapter S corporation with which to run this business? In making your decision as to which entity would be best suited for your business, you should use your tax professional to review the advantages and the disadvantages of each of the entities. If you do select an entity other than the sole-ownership, and the IRS does find that you are not reporting all of your income, you are not able to tell the judge that you can not answer the questions from the IRS due to self-incrimination.

When beginning your business, remember to keep everything in the business as simple as possible. Then as your business grows, you can begin to move into more complex business structures and dealings. For instance, if you begin your business as a sole-owner and do not have any employees, there is no reason to apply for a federal identification number. Just use your social security number for all purposes. The more paper work and tax forms that you send to the IRS, the more likelihood that the IRS will pull one of your documents for audit or review purposes. The KISS theory should come into play in most all of our business, and that is to Keep It Simple and Short.

Well, if I am going into business, will a partnership or corporation save me a lot of taxes? We all have heard that these types of business structures give us the best tax breaks. However, most tax professionals will be quick to tell you that there are only a very few tax advantages to either of these two business structures, and the tax savings will generally not be more than the extra cost of administering these types of business structures. A limited liability partnership will normally be used to help limit the liability of each of the partners in a partnership. A corporation is usually recommended for a business that may present a large liability exposure to the owners. If the business owners want to be taxed as a partnership but have the liability protection of a corporation, then a sub-chapter S corporation can be used. The regular corporation structure, unlike other business structures, will allow you to take deductions for the owners and officers on group medical insurance, disability insurance, and a limited amount of term life insurance. There are some other plans and benefits that a corporation can set up. However, due to the high cost of the plans and the plan administration expense, many corporations are using only the insurance plans.

The sub-chapter S corporation is used many times to distribute income to the owners without their having to pay social security and medicare taxes. If a reasonable amount of the income distributed from the corporation is not distributed as W-2 income, and social security and medicare taxes paid thereon, then the IRS upon auditing the corporation may reclassify some of the income that has been distributed and have these taxes paid. Because of the small number of returns being audited, many taxpayers have become aggressive in distributing this income from these sub-chapter S corporations, and they are not paying the social security and medicare taxes.

The sub-chapter S corporation is also being used extensively by business owners who are between the ages of 62 and 69 years of age. Through this they are able to receive distributions from the corporation and also to begin drawing social security benefits. Most of these taxpayers will draw W-2 income up to the maximum amount allowed by the social security administration. They will then draw any additional funds as sub-chapter S distributions so that social security benefits will not be reduced. If the taxpayer and his spouse are both in this age bracket, then both are able to receive the W-2 income and the distributed income from the corporation. If audited by the IRS, the same question can be raised as to whether more of the income should be distributed as W-2 income.

If I have a regular corporation, when should I elect to change it to a sub-chapter S corporation? Since corporations are taxed at 15% of the first $50,000 of taxable income, most owners want the corporation to pay taxes at this favorable rate and do not elect to be taxed as a sub-chapter S corporation. However, many tax professionals will advise their clients that the sub-chapter S election should be made if the client plans to sale the corporation in four to six years, and the client has a very low cost basis in his corporate stock. By making this election, the corporate owner will be able to increase his basis in the corporation each year as the income of the sub-chapter S corporation is passed through and taxed on his personal tax return. This will reduce the two tiers of taxes that the corporate owner will have to pay upon the sale of his business. The first tier of taxes is paid by the corporation on the gain from the sale of the corporate assets. The second tier of taxes is paid by the corporate owner as liquidating dividend distributions. This is usually at the 28% capital gains rate plus the related state income taxes on all distributions above the owners cost basis.

Another type of corporation that needs to be discussed is the professional association or professional corporation. These are sometimes referred to as a PA or PC, depending on the state in which they are incorporated. These corporations are used by doctors, lawyers, accountants, and other professional businesses. The advantages to these types of corporations are generally the same as for other types of corporations except that in many states these corporations do not limit the professional owner's liability in a malpractice suit. Also, another big disadvantage to these corporations is that the first dollar of net income is taxed at the 35% bracket. Therefore, it is very important that the corporate owner distributes all of the net income each year to avoid this high tax bracket. Most will agree that even if the taxpayer is in the

39.6% bracket, he should distribute this income so that two tiers of taxes will not have to be paid thereon.

Whichever corporate structure you decide to use, you should consider issuing your company stock as restrictive stock so that you can control the ownership of the stock. A family member may own a portion of the stock and through a divorce, a non-family member may end up with the stock if it has not been issued as restricted stock. Usually, the restrictive stock agreement tells who can buy the stock and how much will be paid for the stock by those who will be buying it. These provisions can sometimes be beneficial when assigning a value for this stock for estate tax purposes.

Also, if you decide to use the corporate structure for your business, you should be sure that your attorney sets your corporation up under section 1244 of the Internal Revenue Code. Then if your business is not successful, you will be able to deduct all of your investment in the original stock purchased as a loss in one year. Otherwise, your loss could be limited to $3,000 per year for several years.

Should I form a corporation for each of my business branches or ventures? If some of your business ventures carry a high amount of liability exposure, you may consider using separate corporations for them. Many business branches and ventures can be operated by the same corporation. If your attorney does not recommend that you form a separate corporation because of liability exposure, I suggest that you keep it simple and operate with just one corporation. By having only one corporation, you will have only one set of payroll reports and W-2s to file with the IRS. You will also have only one corporate return to file. Again, the fewer reports and tax returns that you file with the IRS, the less likelihood that your return will be audited.

Many taxpayers will say that they are going to get into the farming business to save taxes. Most of these taxpayers are getting into the cattle or horse raising business without giving much consideration as to how much money will be required to start the farming operation in comparison to the amount of taxes that will be saved. Many taxpayers will make a decision to purchase a $15,000 to $20,000 tractor or other piece of farm equipment since most of it can be written off in the year of purchase. However, many times the taxpayer is in a 15% tax bracket for federal tax and around a 5% tax bracket for state tax; therefore, only $3,000 will be saved in taxes if a $15,000 tractor or other piece of equipment is purchased. The taxpayer will be funding the remaining $12,000 of this purchase out of his earnings. In such cases, the tax professional will usually advise the taxpayer to purchase these items only if they are needed for the farming operations. If the taxpayer is in a 28% or higher bracket for federal purposes, and especially the 39.6% bracket, then the decision to buy new or additional equipment is made easier because taxes pay for nearly 50% of the purchase price. Before getting into farming or other businesses just to save taxes, you need to give much consideration to the amount of cash that you will have to put into the business, over and above the amount of taxes that will be saved. Some of these business ventures can truly fall under the category of being "penny wise and dollar foolish".

For farming businesses, as of January 1, 1989, the depreciation method was changed to the Alternative Depreciation System (ADS). This reduced farm related depreciation from the 200 percent declining balance method to the 150 percent declining balance method. The depreciation life was also increased on most farm assets. The depreciation life for cattle was increased from 5 years to 7 years, and for farm equipment and machinery the depreciation life increased from 7 years to 10 years. Since this reduced farm depreciation considerably, you must consider this if you are planning to start a farming business.

Another important thing to remember when setting up a farming operation is that the IRS may declare your farming venture as a hobby and disallow any losses that you sustain. You must show a profit at least two out of five years if you have a cattle farm and two out of seven years if you have a horse farm. Since many of the large cattle, horse, and row crop farmers do not show a profit for maybe one in five to ten years, the IRS does not hold fast to these rules if the taxpayer continues to show a profit motive in their pursuit of these farming operations.

Over the past five to ten years, many people have set up businesses selling cosmetics, cookware, jewelry, specialty clothing lines, interior home decor and household supplies and cleaning goods. These businesses usually come complete with selling kits, supplies and formal bookkeeping forms to keep up with all of your sales, purchases, expenses and mileage. Because of the large amount of expenses involved in buying products for demonstrations, attending sales meetings, and operating a vehicle, many of these businesses do not show a profit, and many IRS agents will try to disallow your losses if your return is selected for audit. I have found that the IRS may state that they are going to disallow all losses because they do not feel that the taxpayer has a profit motive in conducting these businesses. But when the audit is completed, the losses are generally allowed if you have done a good job documenting all your expenses.

As more and more families have both husband and wife

working, service type businesses have had a big increase. Some are the home cleaning services, fast food and other food services, child care, laundry, bakeries, repair and remodeling, gardening and lawn care, and many types of recreational service businesses. Many of these service businesses operate as sole-owner type businesses, as many of them are small and are operated mostly by one or two individuals. Since many of these businesses are able to operate with very little overhead expenses, the owners are able to produce more profit each year, as their services are being demanded by more and more consumers. In these service type businesses, most of the receipts are by cash. This tempts these owners to under report income for sales tax purposes, as well as for income tax purposes. If these taxpayers do not become overly aggressive in under reporting income, then it is very difficult for the IRS and other taxing authorities to make this determination during an audit.

There have been many combinations of the sell and service businesses also springing up in the last few years. These include the computer business, all types of electronics businesses, and probably the biggest of all, the cellular telephone and paging business.

Another big business that has been gaining momentum in the past two to three years is automobile leasing. We have all heard from the automobile salesperson that if we will just lease a vehicle, we will be able to deduct all of the lease payment on our tax returns. Many of the sales people are telling the buying public this, even though the vehicle is not going to be used in any type of business. Leasing a vehicle will sometimes give you a small tax advantage; however, there is not a simple rule of thumb to follow when making a decision as to whether to buy or lease.

There are some very important points to consider. If you are going to drive your business vehicle over 15,000 miles per year during the lease term, you will probably have to pay the leasing company twelve to fifteen cents per mile for all miles driven over the 15,000 miles. Also many of these vehicles require a major up front payment to the leasing company even though the monthly advertised lease payment is quit low. Since you do not build any equity in the leased vehicle and you may get soaked with high mileage charges, you should consult your tax professional when making a decision on whether to lease or buy your business vehicle.

Many other leasing companies have also become very large and lease all types of equipment such as computers, copy machines, fork lifts, and other industrial machinery. Most of these leases are lease-purchases, and after all payments are paid to the leasing company, the equipment becomes the property of the lessee. The lease payments are generally written off as lease expense as paid by the business. However, if the IRS audits, they may determine that your lease is in fact a lease-purchase and require you to depreciate the equipment rather than take a lease expense deduction. Unless you have a large amount of leased equipment, the lease expense deduction will probably not flag your return.

Whether the businesses that we have discussed are small sole-owner businesses or large corporate businesses, all of the business dealings are controlled or governed by the same Internal Revenue Service Codes and Regulations. Since this is the case, why can some of the businesses seem to have a much lesser taxable income than other businesses in a similar trade? The answer to this question can be found in the way the different owners report income and in the way that the owners deduct various expenses.

Many of the owners with lower taxable income will report only a portion of their income, and many owners will deduct expenses that are personal or semi-personal. One of the items that these owners may be deducting is expense on vehicles that are being used for business as well as for personal travel. The businessman may be claiming personal long distant telephone calls, country club and other dues, and convention expenses that are actually family vacations. Often products are deducted as a business expense but are actually being used at home. Sometimes repair and maintenance is paid by the business, but the actual work is done at the taxpayer's home. Of course, if these items are found during an audit, the taxpayer can expect to pay some hefty taxes, penalties, and interest. But with fewer and fewer audits being performed by the IRS, there is now less chance of these taxpayers being caught cheating on their tax returns.

Chapter 4

Illegal Tax Saving Techniques (Please Do Not Attempt to Use Any of These)

THE ILLEGAL TAX SAVING TECHNIQUES IN THIS chapter are for informational purposes only and should not be attempted by anyone. Most of them will either get you put in the federal penitentiary system or at best cost you substantial penalties and will possibly get you checked often by the IRS. The printer, the publishers, and I, as well as others directly or indirectly involved in the production of this book, take no responsibility for your use or attempted use of any of the methods discussed in this chapter and again suggest that you only use legal tax saving techniques in all of your tax planning.

There are tax avoidance and tax evasion schemes that many people are willing to try because most feel that the tax system as we know it is out of control. The federal government is taxing the hard worker at too high a tax rate and then redistributing this wealth to those who are not willing to work but have learned to use the system to generate food stamps, housing allowances, aid to dependent children, free medical care, and the list goes on and on. I usually refer to those that are willing to work and produce income and taxes as "the net producers" and those who use the system to provide them almost everything they have as "the net users". As most of us know "the net users" are swiftly outnumbering "the net producers," and at this fast pace of increase, the "users" will out number and out vote the "producers" within a few short years. It can only be anyone's guess what will happen to society as we know it today when this eventually happens. The "producers" will no longer have any incentive left to want to produce for the "users". Hopefully, our elected officials and we as voters will be able to turn the tide before this day of reckoning arrives and destroys our society.

Filing as Exempt or Showing too Many Exemptions on Form W-4

There have been many employees in the construction industries and the automobile assembly business that have been showing a large number of dependents on their forms W-4 to reduce the amount of federal and state income taxes withheld accordingly. Also, some have filed these payroll tax withholding forms as the taxpayer's being exempt from income tax withholding. When an employee shows ten or more exemptions on their W-4 form or files these forms as exempt, the employer is required to notify the IRS that the employee has filed such a form. However, most employers do not know that the IRS is supposed to be notified about such filings and are therefore subjecting themselves to some large penalties because of this lack of knowledge on their part.

After filing these large number of dependents or as being exempt on these W-4 forms, the taxpayer is generally having no federal or state income tax withheld and is merely then not filing tax returns at the end of each year. One may ask why the IRS is not able to police or control this better than what is being done. The answer is that there is such a large number of taxpayers doing this. The IRS is just overwhelmed by the numbers, and sometimes it may take them many years to target a taxpayer or a group of taxpayers in a particular industry or industry classification.

In recent years, when the IRS does finally target a particular industry where many taxpayers are using these methods, the IRS will usually bring in many agents to the related industry. They will check all taxpayers, and all who are not in compliance with the filing of this form will be heavily penalized. In many cases the IRS has actually requested and has been granted jail time for those that have used these methods. This has happened in some instances when only a few hundred or a few thousand dollars of taxes were owed by the taxpayer.

In other cases, taxpayers have owed many thousands of dollars when checked for some other reasons, and the IRS has not requested the same large penalties or jail time for them. The reader may wonder why the taxpayer who actually owes less taxes was treated more harshly. I have wondered the same thing in many cases that I have known about and have actually asked agents the reasoning they use in making the decision for the large penalties and jail time for the different taxpayers. The answers that most agents give concerning these large penalties and jail time is publicity. By moving into a particular industry where many taxpayers are using these particular abusive tax methods and sending a large number of individuals to the federal penitentiary system at the same time, the IRS is able to get a lot of newspaper, television, and radio coverage. With this widespread publicity, the IRS is able to strike fear into other taxpayers who may be thinking about using the same methods of avoiding or evading the tax system. This fear of the IRS may not be the only thing that makes many of us try to file a return that is accurate, but most of the time this fear is the controlling factor in making us file an accurate return.

Dealing in Cash and the Underground Economy

The IRS tells the public that it is using a particular audit approach or technique to catch drug dealers or the mob who are only dealing in cash transactions. In fact most of these audit procedures will be used only when performing audits on the average taxpayer and will never catch the first drug dealer or mob member. Most red-blooded American taxpayers would like to see the IRS or any other governmental agency catch, prosecute, and throw away the key on every drug dealer and every mob member in the United States. However, these individuals usually have better run businesses than the Fortune 500 companies, and for sure are able to structure anything they do to keep from having any problems with the IRS and most other governmental agencies.

In recent years, the IRS has been proposing to change the color of our currency from green to some other color. Then the drug dealers, money counterfeiters, or mob members will not be able to use any of the cash bills that they have printed or accumulated over a period of time. They propose that after announcing that the dollars are going to be changed, we will be able to go into our bank in the next 30 to 60 days and exchange up to $5,000 to $10,000 of our green cash for other color bills being issued.

While this may sound good, there are also problems. Many of our older taxpayers have a large amount of cash on hand for many different reasons. However, if you ask them, most will tell you that they once lost money during the depression or in the most recent savings and loan scandals that rocked the American economy, and they do not trust banks. They keep these funds so that they will not lose everything they have should the American economy have another depression. These older taxpayers have generally paid all of the taxes due on these funds and would have much difficulty in converting their cash from one color to another. They would probably not be able to convert all of their funds because of the stringent guidelines that they would have to follow in converting the cash.

The drug dealers and mob members, on the other hand, would be able to convert most or all of their cash because of the elaborate network that they usually keep in place to handle situations such as this. Again, the unknowing and law abiding taxpayer will pay dearly for this IRS directive if congress ever permits this cash conversion to take place. The money counterfeiters may not be able to convert any of their counterfeit bills into the new currency, but will merely make new printing plates for any changes made in these new bills and will print new counterfeit bills using the new color that is selected by the IRS directive.

Just how big is the underground economy in the United States? Many IRS agents contend that the underground economy is 5% to 6% of the total economy; however, I believe the underground economy to be much larger and to be growing each year. There are many reasons that the underground economy is growing. The primary reason for the continued growth is that most taxpayers consider the system to be out of control, and they are being soaked with taxes to pay for many things that they think are totally unreasonable for the government to be funding. Therefore, the taxpayer begins to deal in cash for some or all of his transactions so as to be able to eliminate or reduce part of his tax liability.

What part of the underground economy is growing the fastest? Without considering the large underground economy that is being conducted by drug dealers, one of the fastest growing underground economy is being conducted by foreigners that are entering the United States. Some of these foreigners are entering the country legally; however, many are in the country illegally. Many of the dollars that these foreigners are earning are being sent back to their families in their home country and are not only evading our taxes, but are also helping to further upset our balance of trade. Many of these foreigners live in California and have developed successful businesses which are fully driven by cash sales. It appears that the IRS continues to lose ground in their effort to curtail this type of underground economy.

Illegal Schemes Involving Sports

Recently another underground scheme involved sports. Some well known retired baseball stars were sentenced for tax fraud for their participation in a 1989 sports memorabilia autograph show in Atlantic City, New Jersey. They were each paid by cash, and the cash payment was never reported as income on their tax returns. The lucrative sports memorabilia business had featured eleven baseball players who had 500 or more home runs during their careers in the major leagues. One of the former players admitted receiving $10,000 in unreported cash at this function and admitted receiving more than $100,000 cash over a ten year period. No taxes had been paid on the income. Another former player admitted receiving cash of $33,000 at this same function and almost $70,000 over a three year period. The IRS stated that other former baseball stars were still being investigated, and that their investigation of the sports memorabilia business was being expanded into other sports and sport businesses. In cases such a this, living a high profile life and being well known to the public makes you more likely to have your business dealings scrutinized closely by the IRS.

Other Dealings in Cash

There are many ways that taxpayers deal in cash to avoid or evade taxes. Most of the dealings involve paying cash for goods and services or selling goods and services for cash, and not ringing up the sale in any cash register. Therefore, no state sales tax, no state income tax, nor any federal income tax is paid on these funds.

Does the IRS have any audit techniques and procedures in place to check for these cash transactions? You can bet your bottom dollar that this is one of the audit techniques and procedures each agent will use on all of their audits. One of the first things that the IRS agent will check is if the taxpayer has paid out or received more than $10,000 in a single cash transaction or in a combination of cash transactions dealing with a particular customer. If such cash transactions are handled by a taxpayer, he is supposed to report this transaction to the IRS on Form 8300 and report a great deal of information about the person paying the cash as well as the reason for the transaction. If this is not reported to the IRS, the penalty can be equal to the cash transaction not reported to the IRS.

Many taxpayers do not even know that this reporting requirement has been around for many years and are therefore not reporting these transactions. They are surprised when the agent proposes many thousand dollars of penalties for not properly reporting these transactions. Since this can be a combination of transactions and not just a single transaction, a business can still be caught in this penalty trap. For example, one employee may receive part of the cash and then another employee may receive the balance of the transaction many days later without ever knowing that the first transaction has taken place.

If you are a taxpayer and are trying to pay most of your taxes due, you should protect yourself in these situations. Tell those who are trying to pass a large amount of cash through your business that you report all transactions over the $10,000 to the IRS as required. Inform them that you will be glad to sell your goods or services to them but will in no way jeopardize your business with the penalties that can accrue because of these types of transactions.

Another audit procedure and technique that the IRS uses to check for those that may be dealing in cash and not reporting all of their income is a procedure called the t-account method of accounting for all of your income and expenses. The agent will list all of your expenses and cash pay outs, both personal and business on the right side of the t-account. All of your income and cash receipts, both personal and business are listed on the left side of the t-account. If the expense and cash pay out side of the t-account exceeds the income and cash receipt side of your t-account for the year, the IRS will consider that this is unreported income for the year being audited. If you cannot show that these excess funds are from bank loans or from some other non taxable source, then the agent will assess these excess funds to you as additional taxable income. The taxpayer will find that disproving these t-accounts is very difficult if the agent has prepared the t-account correctly. However, many of the t-accounts prepared by the agents are full of errors, and the taxpayer will usually have to depend on a tax return professional to determine where the errors exists and to prove to the agent that the errors do appear on their t-account. Many times when these errors are corrected, the tax being proposed may not be due. Even though this is a method that all IRS agents are taught as one of their primary methods of auditing for unreported income, even the most seasoned agents often make errors when preparing these t-accounts.

Many times a taxpayer begins to do some dealing in cash and does not get checked by the IRS for several years. The taxpayer may get braver and braver in their cash dealings and also become lax in remembering what to do with the cash and what not to do with the cash. Most taxpayers realize that none of the money can be deposited in the bank and none of the cash can be used to pay bank loans or any other type of notes. If the cash is deposited or if a note payment is made, then the IRS will discover this cash whenever they do the t-account during your audit. Many taxpayers who deal in cash know that there are only a few things for which this cash can be used. These include buying clothes, furniture, and other personal items, as well as taking trips, placing funds in tax free bonds or tax free mutual funds, buying gold and silver coins, making contributions to your church or other charitable organizations, contributing to political campaigns, and, of course the age old device of placing the cash funds in your lock box.

In some cases, taxpayers have been caught by the IRS spending cash. For example, when a taxpayer and spouse are making a trip, either one or the other may have the bad habit of pulling a credit card or check out to pay for an item. The IRS will then have a paper trail to place them on this out of town trip.

Investments can also be a problem. When buying tax free bonds, as well as tax free mutual funds, the taxpayer often wants to use his regular broker. When he is audited by the IRS, the IRS merely asks the brokerage firm for all transactions for this taxpayer. These transactions will also show up at this time; therefore, to avoid this problem most taxpayers will buy these tax free instruments from a broker with whom they do no other transactions.

Of course, the way to get caught by the IRS when keeping your cash in your bank lock box is easy. When the IRS agent asks you if you have a lock box, he then may request that you open the lock box in his presence. Most taxpayers will remove any cash, and any gold and silver coins from their lock box immediately upon receiving the notice from the IRS that they are going to be audited.

The IRS has an information collection center in most service centers and area offices called "clip and save". These collection centers are responsible for reviewing articles in news papers and other news data and clipping and saving anything that the IRS considers important for audit or collection purposes. For example, when taxpayers go deep sea fishing or go on a cruise, they usually have pictures made. It is very tempting to give some of these pictures to your local newspaper so that all of your friends can see the large sail fish that you have caught or the good time that you had. If you have used your untaxed cash to make these trips, you are providing the IRS the necessary information to tax this cash. If you are dealing in cash, you must keep a low profile and play everything low key to keep from having to pay tax on this cash at a later time. You should share this kind of information with only your very close friends.

You must also be careful reporting stolen goods. You may have something stolen from your home or business and that item had been purchased with cash. You, of course, have a tendency to tell the local law enforcement agencies what has been stolen and the amount that the stolen goods have cost. The local law enforcement agencies report this information directly to the local newspaper which is then read by the IRS. Therefore, before reporting these items, you must make a decision as to whether you will report the amount for insurance purposes to the law enforcement agencies or if you should avoid reporting the information, so that the IRS will not be able to gather this information.

Another cash transaction that has steadily gained momentum in the last four to five years is the slotting fees that a grocery store chain or other chain stores charge a wholesaler to place their goods on the store shelves. The higher the slotting fee, the more prominent place and space is made available in the retail stores for the salable food and other products. These slotting fees are now making their way into the small local grocery stores, hardware stores, and other merchandisers. In some cases, this slotting fee is being reported as income on the individual business tax return. However, more and more of the businesses are requesting these slotting fees in cash. Many of them go untaxed, and it appears that the IRS has not developed a very good audit procedure to detect these unreported cash transactions.

Bartering Transactions

What are bartering transactions? One of the things that an IRS agent asks when he is interviewing a taxpayer is whether or not you are involved in any bartering transactions. If you tell the agent that you are involved in bartering transactions, it seems to put the agent into a tale spin, and he seems to have problems responding to this answer. Bartering is simply the process of the taxpayer trading his goods and services for the goods and services of someone else.

There are many bartering exchanges of which one can become a member, and all of the related transactions are properly reported to the IRS. These types of bartering exchanges are merely methods of increasing your business without the exchange of payment by check or credit card. They are in no way an attempt to try to keep from paying any related taxes that may be due on these transactions.

The bartering transactions that the IRS is trying to delve into are those where a taxpayer will exchange his goods or services for the goods or services of another without their being properly reported to the IRS. An example of this type of bartering would be an attorney or medical doctor who exchanges his services for furniture or automobile repairs. Also, a retailer may exchange his goods for dental work or some other goods from another retailer. If this type of bartering is not done in excess, then the IRS usually has trouble determining that any type of bartering transactions are taking place. The IRS can catch these if the agent begins to review a doctor's or dentist's appointment or day book and then compares the patient's names to the individual account receivable ledger card or to daily detailed deposits. He may observe that credits are posted to ledger cards and the related credit is not shown on the daily detailed deposit slip. This is usually prevented by not posting these bartering transactions with other transactions and by keeping the patient's ledger cards out of the regular ledger card tray. Also, another common method used to find these transactions is for the IRS agent to ask one of your employees, when you are either not present or when they call your office, if you conduct any type of these transactions. Many employees think that they have to answer any and all questions that these agents ask regardless of the consequences to either themselves or to their employers. As I discuss in another chapter of this book, never, never let an IRS agent perform the audit in your home or office. Always instruct your employees that if an IRS agent or any tax agent calls your office they are to give out no information, and if the agent keeps insisting or tries to intimidate the employee to give information to them, instruct the employee to hang up and not talk with the agent any further.

Changing Businesses to Evade Taxes

Some taxpayers are beginning businesses and are not paying all of the required payroll and other IRS and state taxes. The taxpayers may be able to operate the first business for several months or even up to two years before an IRS collection agent appears at the business and attempts to collect any taxes due. The IRS agent may allow the business to operate for another 5 to 6 months before the agent actually closes the business. These taxpayers may then begin another business in the same location or town using another name. If they are not able to get a new federal identification number using the taxpayer's name, they will merely change the federal identification application to the spouse's name, and they are in business again. If the spouse is denied a federal identification number, then the taxpayer may apply for the new number in one of their children's names, or even change their business to a partnership or a corporation. This process may be repeated several times in the same location or town. Once the IRS has determined that these taxpayers have continued to evade taxes using these methods, the taxpayers move to another town or another section of the United States.

This scam of not paying taxes may continue for many years before the IRS is finally able to keep these taxpayers from the continual evasion of taxes by tracking their application for new federal identification numbers. To prevent this abuse, the IRS is now quickly following up when a taxpayer does not make their payroll tax deposits or other tax deposits on a timely basis. Also, if taxpayers are changing their form of business from a sole-ownership or partnership to a corporation, the IRS has started to review some of these applications in detail to determine if there are any taxes owed by the former business.

Evasive Use of Earned Income Credit

The earned income credit or negative income tax is being claimed by taxpayers who have income that does not exceed the upper mid twenty thousand dollars and who have a dependent living with them. In many cases, this negative income tax is being paid back to some taxpayers who do not even have income taxes withheld. This is costing the government billions of dollars each year. The cost of this negative income tax for those that do actually qualify for the credit is already many billion dollars.

However, there are many taxpayers that have learned how to manipulate their income and manipulate a dependent deduction so that they will show that they qualify for this credit. They can expect to receive back over two thousand dollars. So many have learned how to do this manipulation that the IRS attempted to close this flood gate during the 1994 filing season by delaying paying many of these credit amounts until the taxpayers proved that they met all of the filing requirements for claiming this credit. Many of these credits have been processed by electronic tax return filers, and the taxpayers have been receiving these funds quickly by using the refund anticipation loans that many of these electronic tax return preparers offer.

This abuse is so wide spread that the IRS attempted to get congress to double all tax return preparer penalties in the 1995 Budget Reconciliation Act. It appears that the IRS is trying to shift the "policing" of the abusive use of this credit from themselves to the tax return preparers.

This negative income tax and government give-away is considered a form of welfare payment to those that qualify. If you feel that welfare payments such as this should be administered by a government agency other than the IRS, you should let your congressman know. If tax fraud and welfare fraud were eradicated, we would probably be the only nation in the world without debt, and would for sure have the lowest income taxes.

Estates

If an estate has less than the $600,000 exemption amount, and an estate tax return does not have to be filed, executors may leave the estate open for four or five years. In these estates, the CDs and other investments usually will amount to no more than $150,000. The income that had been produced by these CDs and other investments had not been large enough to make the deceased taxpayer have to file and pay income taxes. When the executor leaves the estate open, he also will leave the social security number of the deceased taxpayer on these items so that the Form 1099 will continue to reflect that the income belongs to the deceased taxpayer. Even though taxes are generally owed on all income of $600 or more on these estates, it appears that the IRS does not have a very good system in place to detect this tactic.

If an estate is $700,000 to $800,000 and is composed mostly of real estate, some executors will attempt to get appraisals or value estimates reduced to the $600,000 exemption amount so that an estate tax return will not have to be filed. This sounds good, unless the assets in the estate are going to be sold by the recipients within a few years. The estate will probably pay less in estate taxes on the higher valuations than the recipients will have to pay because of the lower valuations.

If you decide to use some form of illegal tax evasion techniques that have been discussed in this chapter or others that are continually tried by taxpayers, what is the possibility that the IRS will be able to detect your tax evasion scheme? Five or six years ago, it would have been more probable that the IRS would be able to detect these tax evasion schemes, than they are able to currently. In the past, if someone called an IRS office, or IRS employee, and reported that a business or an individual taxpayer was using tax evasion schemes or was not properly paying payroll or other taxes, an effort was made by the IRS to determine if this information was correct. If the information was correct, the IRS would pursue anyone not paying the proper taxes. Presently, if an agent is not working directly on the audit examination on which someone has reported some wrong doing, the information will probably not amount to anything except a wasted phone call from the individual making the call. In some cases, the IRS may receive several telephone calls from different individuals about the same business or taxpayer and will still not act on the information. It appears that the IRS agents do not want to work on or pursue anything that the individual agent has not developed through his own actions or audit procedures. Most of the IRS agents just do not want to rock the IRS Company "boat" and will not take the initiative to pursue anything on their own. At the present time, if someone threatens you with calling the IRS to report something that you are doing, you may have the urge to give them the local or district IRS telephone number and invite them to make the call. However, I suggest that you let this urge pass.

I again strongly suggest that you only use legal methods of tax planning and under no circumstances should you attempt to use any of the things discussed in this chapter.

In the example section of this book, the Department of the Treasury Notice 746 has been reprinted to show the large number of penalties and interest that are now being charged by the IRS for everything from filing and paying late to fraud. The penalties are number 01 to number 58, and many of them apply to the things that have been discussed in this chapter. Also, please note that the IRS charges you 1% more interest expense than they pay to you when an overpayment is due to you. Even with these large numbers of penalties and the large amount of the penalties, the IRS is still losing their on-going battle of getting the taxpayer to file and pay their taxes when due.

Chapter 5

How to Select a CPA or Other Tax Advisor

SAVING TAXES AND BUILDING YOUR WEALTH WILL be very dependent on the CPA or any other tax advisor that you select. Many CPAs and other tax advisors become too technical for many taxpayers and cannot identify with the individual taxpayer's needs. Selecting the CPA or tax advisor who is best for you can be time consuming and frustrating; however, I have included several items in this chapter to help you in making your selection.

Do I Need a CPA?

If you have W-2s and a few itemized deductions, you should be able to complete your own return and not require the assistance of a CPA or other tax professional. However, if you have a business, farm, rental property, or sale of property, you should consider using a CPA or other tax professional. Usually the taxes saved from using a CPA will be more than the fees that you will pay for the services of the CPA. Having your return prepared by a professional will also give you some piece of mind, since fewer professionally prepared returns are checked by the IRS.

Do I Need a Big Six CPA Firm?

The big six CPA firms are generally very impersonal unless you or your company have some very deep pockets, and you do not mind how much you spend for tax advice or tax return preparation fees. Unless you are a very large client, you are usually assigned to one of the younger individuals in the firm and may never meet or talk with one of the tax managers or tax partners. If you do have a tax problem that requires having a manager or partner to review, the big firms will usually contact their national office for tax research and further tax advice. By doing this, they saddle you with at least a three tier layer of very high hourly employees and your billing is usually three times what you had estimated it would be.

These big six firms hire a new "crop" of individuals each year from all of the major colleges and universities. They usually hire from the top 5% of the graduating class, and many times these students have a master of accounting degree or other advanced degrees. What must be remembered is that even though these students are the "cream of the crop," they still must be trained in the work-a-day world. Even though they have some very good academic credentials, they may require two to three years to be able to represent you before the IRS or other taxing authorities. They will have to be trained on your account and on other clients' accounts.

After these employees have been trained, fifty percent or more leave these big six firms, open firms of their own, or go to work for the client. With this process repeating itself, new employees have to be trained to do your tax work on a continuing basis, and it is hard for these big six firms to keep someone on their staff that is totally familiar with your business and your individual tax situations.

Some of the larger banks have the "big six" mentality and insist that if you borrow from their banks, you must use a big six firm for an audit or tax work. If this is the case, you may have to dig deep into your pockets to be able to accommodate your banker's wishes. If your banker has this "big six" mentality, you might consider changing banks. Then you will have the ability to select your own CPA firm that can better meet your current and future tax needs because they do not have to train their new employees year after year.

I worked with a Big Six CPA firm for several years after graduating from college. By working with one of these firms, an accountant has the benefit of being exposed to many different businesses over a very short period of time. This helps him make a decision about the type of business with which he eventually wants to work. I still work jointly with some of these firms on business acquisitions and on audits. I have also worked in litigation support with the Big Six firm representing the other side. When working with this litigation support, I am always pleased to oppose a Big Six partner from some distant location rather than a regional or local CPA. Most of these Big Six employees have a general knowledge of the subject matter, but they do not have specific knowledge. As with myself, many of the Big Six employees know that they will stay with these firms for four or five years and will then go to work for one of their clients.

Do I Need a Local or Regional CPA Firm?

There are many local and regional CPA firms in the larger cities throughout the USA. The regional firms may have two to twenty different offices in different cities and states. These regional firms usually specialize in different areas of the economy such as construction, trucking, oil & gas, banking, government, non-profit, and manufacturing audit and tax related work. These regional firms differ from the big six firms as they usually have a more personal contact with their clients. Their employees tend to stay after they have been with the firm for two or three years. A big factor with the regional firms is that their fees usually are as much as 25% less than the rates of the big six firms. The regional firms should definitely be considered when making your decision on your tax advisor.

The local CPA firms usually range from a one person office with a secretary to 30 to 40 CPAs with 10 to 15 support employees including secretaries. While some of these firms are very large, most of the firms specialize in different audit and tax areas as do the regional firms. These local firms usually give very personal attention to their clients and usually do not have much employee turn-over after an employee has been with the firm for two to three years. Also, the staff of these local firms are cross trained on the work of many of the clients. Since other staff members are familiar with your particular tax problems, you can call the firm and get an answer to a tax question without waiting until the person in charge of your account gets back into the office.

A big factor to consider when selecting a local firm is that their fees usually are as much as 50% less than the rates of the big six firms. Since the personal attention is much better with the local firms and the fees are more reasonable, I suggest that you seek out a local firm, unless you are required by your bank or others to use a big six or a regional firm.

Do I Need a Tax Attorney?

Most tax attorneys prepare very few tax returns, but generally they represent clients before IRS appeals, tax court, or in criminal investigation division audits performed by the IRS. Most CPAs get their clients to hire a tax attorney if it appears that an IRS case is headed to tax court or if a client is being audited by the criminal investigation division of the IRS. CPAs also use tax attorneys to draft documents for estate planning for clients as well as probating estates for deceased taxpayers.

When you do use a tax attorney to probate an estate, always be sure to ask if you will be billed on an hourly basis or as a percentage of the gross estate. If the percentage of the gross estate is used in billing an estate, the client is usually left speechless for several days after receiving the bill. Let your CPA decide when you need to hire a tax attorney, and be sure your CPA is present when you first meet with the tax attorney. The CPA will help establish your cost of hiring the tax attorney, and the CPA can share information with the tax attorney. Then the work will not be performed and paid for two times.

What Questions Do I Ask When Selecting My CPA?

To select my CPA, do I simply go to the yellow pages of my phone book and select a firm at random, do I select one that has an impressive sounding name, or do I use some other approach?

I suggest that you ask many questions when selecting your CPA. Are your friends who have similar companies or tax problems pleased with the job that their CPA is doing for them? You need to ask these friends the strong points as well as the weak points of the CPA that they are using. Be sure to ask them if they get the personal attention that they need from their CPA and if the firm has sufficient professional staff. Talk with as many different friends as possible about their CPA firm. At least talk with five or six friends when trying to develop the strong points and the weak points of the different firms. Often, you will find that one or two firms will be used by these five or six friends. If this is the case, you may only need to talk with the one or two firms in making your final decision.

When meeting with the prospective CPA firms you should ask at least the following questions:

(A) Does your CPA firm have sufficient staff so that I can get the personal attention that I need?

(B) Will more than one staff member be familiar with my business so that I can get questions answered without having to wait several days?

(C) Will I be able to meet with and discuss important items

with partners and managers in the firm when the need arises and on a continuing basis?
(D) What amount of employee turn-over does the firm experience, and do you expect any immediate turn-over in the employees you assign to my account or tax problem?
(E) Does the firm have the expertise in my field so that I can be advised on a continuing basis about tax planning that will help to give me the lowest tax payments possible?
(F) What has the firm's experience been in representing clients before the IRS and other taxing authorities?
(G) What success rate has the firm experienced in the tax cases that they have handled?
(H) How long has the firm been in business, and is the firm financially sound?

Some economists are telling us that by the year 2000, most professional organizations such as CPAs and attorneys will either be very large or very small, and that the medium size firms will either be merged into larger firms or will cease to be. I believe that there will continue to be mergers of the larger firms as well as the regional and local firms. However; with the regional and local firms usually having lower overhead and therefore lower hourly billing rates, these regional and local firms will continue to grow as long as the owners change with the times and technology. These changes and mergers in the next few years should also be considered when making your selection of the CPA firm that your business will use.

Chapter 6

Taxpayer Salvation and Required Changes in the Tax System

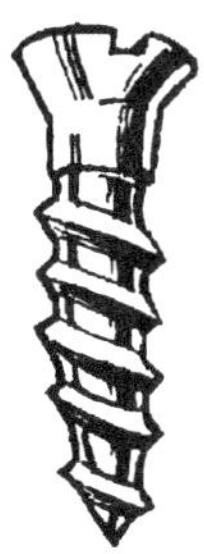

THE FIRST INCOME TAX WAS ASSESSED IN 1861 to help finance the costs of the civil war, and then it was abolished in 1872. The tax was again implemented in 1894 and then found to be unconstitutional in 1895 by the U. S. Supreme Court. The sixteenth amendment to the constitution was ratified in 1913, and congress then passed an income-tax system that is still with us today.

The current tax system is at the least very cumbersome and is very hard for most everyone to understand. This includes the IRS agents. The system has been added to, changed, modified, and every few years completely revised. The whole code and regulations are often changed to try to help some politicians alter some social or economic condition that they believe exists and can be immediately cured by making these enormous changes in our taxing system. Those making these many changes are usually attorneys who work for the IRS national office in

Washington, D. C., and most of the code and regulation changes are therefore so technical that no one other than tax professionals such as CPAs and tax attorneys could be expected to understand them.

Since most believe that the current tax system is out of control and out of date, many proposals are being made to make radical changes in the tax collecting system as we know it today. Some are proposing to have a simple flat tax with few to no deductions for the taxpayers. The taxpayers would simply file a small computer card size form listing their gross income and any deductions allowed for personal exemptions and other standard or itemized deductions. Then the tax would be calculated at a flat tax rate of 15% to 17%. This flat tax proposal sounds very simple and, of course, would do away with the complex IRS code and regulations that we have today. However, this flat tax proposal does not address the need or any method to overcome the underground economy that has continued to increase each year. The flat tax would give the IRS agents additional time to pursue those who are dealing in cash transactions and those who have dropped off the tax paying roles completely. With this flat tax proposal the IRS would probably be able to downsize by 50%, and the need for professional tax return preparers would drop accordingly.

When the flat tax proposal is discussed by the political leaders, it really sounds very inviting and appears to be the direction that should be pursued for an overhaul of our tax system. However, we basically already have a flat tax system with most of the taxpayers paying a 15% tax rate after deducting our personal exemptions and our standard deduction. Even though some are still able to itemize their deductions, rather than take the standard deduction, fewer and fewer are using itemized deductions each year because of the continued increase in the standard deduction.

Another area that the politicians are not addressing publicly is the social security and medicare taxes that are now costing most of us more in taxes than our income taxes. With the combined social security and medicare taxes costing us and our employers 15.3%, in some cases, we may be paying twice as much in these taxes as we are paying in our regular income taxes. Will the new flat tax rate being proposed include both our income tax and our social security and medicare taxes, or will we still be paying the social security and medicare taxes over and above the flat tax rate? Most of us can surmise that this would be too good to be true, and any time we believe this way, the middle income taxpayer will probably again get soaked with higher taxes rather than lower taxes.

The Value Added Tax (VAT) is another tax that is being proposed by some and is a tax that closely resembles our state sales tax. The tax is added to the wholesale price that a manufacturing company charges to the retail store who will then charge a larger selling price to the consumer who buys the product. If a car manufacturer normally sells an automobile to the dealer for $20,000, and then adds a 10% VAT to this automobile, the dealer would then pay $22,000 for this same automobile and would charge the consumer an additional $2,000 when the automobile was sold. The manufacturer would pay the related VAT tax to the IRS, and the dealer and the consumer would not have to file any returns nor pay any tax to the IRS.

This same method of taxing for other consumer goods would cause the consumer to pay for the passed through VAT tax on all new consumer goods. However, no tax would be charged on used consumer goods. Some argue that the poorer taxpayers would be paying a higher rate of tax with this VAT system of taxation in place, but it must be remembered that the tax would only be charged on new goods and not on used goods. So a consumer who buys a used automobile will not owe any VAT. If food products are not exempted from this tax, the poorer taxpayer will probably pay more tax than he is paying now, but some upward modification in federal assistance for some of the taxpayers will help to overcome any additional tax paid by this group of taxpayers.

There are some areas of the VAT that have not been worked out. One is whether the VAT would be added to services in addition to consumer goods. If services are taxed with the VAT, then these service companies would also have to pay the VAT tax collected to the IRS. Also, will the social security and medicare taxes be collected from the taxpayer in addition to this VAT tax. The question for corporations is whether they will continue to be taxed on profits as they have been taxed in the past and the VAT apply to just consumer goods sold to the individual taxpayers.

Most believe that a 17% to 20% VAT would generate enough tax to run our federal government and replace the federal income tax, and 27% to 30% would be enough to replace the federal income tax as well as the social security and medicare taxes. For each 5% of VAT, there should be taxes collected of approximately $105 billion. One of the biggest savings to the federal government with this VAT tax system is that the IRS should probably be able to reduce their staffs by 50% to 75% and still have enough employees to see that all taxes are being paid accurately. This VAT should also have a corresponding reduction in the need for professional tax return preparers.

This method of taxation would also eliminate the problem of the underground economy, as anyone buying consumer goods with a check, credit card, or with cash would be paying the VAT tax. Therefore, any drug dealer or mob member buying any type of consumer goods would pay this tax at the point of purchase even though he may use cash to make the purchase. By eliminating this underground economy using this VAT tax, we may be able to reduce the national debt each year instead of having it to continue to increase at an alarming rate.

There are 19 out of 23 leading industrialized nations that use the VAT. The VAT is as high as 38% in some of the European countries, and most of these countries have more than doubled their VAT since it was first begun. When you read of countries such as Italy, Britain, and Sweden that have the VAT, it is apparent that the United States taxpayer is paying less in taxes than the citizens of these countries. Our unemployment is generally less than the unemployment in these countries. Even though the need for tax agents should decrease with this tax, there are usually more tax agents in these countries on a per taxpayer basis.

Another proposal is to eliminate most all itemized deductions and raise the standard deduction that can be used by each taxpayer. This is probably the proposal that most politicians prefer, as it will not require a large number of IRS agents being eliminated. Our elected officials just cannot bring themselves to downsize any of the federal government as is being done in all areas of the private sector.

Whether the decision is made to use a flat tax, a value added tax, or eliminate most of the itemized deductions, there is one thing that we can all know for certain. If any changes are made, it will take only a year or two until new changes and revisions will be suggested, and the IRS code will again become as complicated and cumbersome as it is now.

Since some changes will probably be made to the IRS code on a continuing basis, and since these changes will probably not simplify our tax filing and tax paying requirements, the IRS must look for ways to improve their audit techniques and be able to do more auditing and tax collecting using fewer and fewer agents and employees. For the IRS to be able to do this, they will have to be willing to acquire more high tech computer systems and will have to be willing to pay higher salaries to get and keep more qualified agents and employees. In talking with various agents, you will find that the main reason that they are staying with the IRS is not for the pay but for the benefits. As pay and benefits continue to increase in the private sector, many of the more seasoned agents and employees of the IRS will leave the service and find jobs in the private sector.

Many of the IRS agents will tell you that once they are hired by the service, it appears from that day forward that the group managers and other supervisory personnel are trying to find reasons to terminate them. Because of this continual turmoil, the morale within the ranks of the agents usually stays very low. Another demoralizing factor that will take many years to overcome is the close downs of the federal government during November and December 1995.

Also, the pay and retirement varies considerably between the different agent categories within the service. The criminal investigation division agents can retire at age 50, get premium pay, and receive good retirement benefits. However, collection and other agents can retire only after 30 years of service or at age 55 with full benefits. For these agents, there is a movement to raise the retirement age from 55 to 65. Most of these agents know that their average life expectancy is 57 1/2 years, so if an agent retires at age 55, this usually gives them a very short retirement life. The reasoning used to give the CID agents earlier retirement is that their jobs are more stressful because of the type of work they do. Many feel that they have such a dangerous job that they are required to carry guns in their everyday job.

Another problem is safety. Many tax professionals believe that not enough consideration is given to the collection agent's safety. These agents are sent into the field without any protection and are to collect taxes from all types of individuals. They should be able to carry weapons as is permitted by the CID agents. To hire and keep good and professional collection agents, the service is going to have to make the collection agent's job less stressful and safer.

To be able to promote and keep more group managers and supervisors in these jobs, the IRS must increase their salaries to an amount that will encourage experienced agents to seek these jobs. Presently they avoid them because of the small amount of salary increases and many more duties and headaches associated with the job. Most tax professionals know of agents who have served as acting group managers or supervisors but have refused to take the job permanently. They refused because of the small increase in salary or because of the possibility of being moved or transferred to another service center location or job. If these positions had more pay and job stability, then we would see more seasoned agents move into these jobs. This would boost the morale within the service. It would give each office location the management and technical depth that is needed for new employee-training as well as enable them to work with the tax professionals and the taxpayers.

One of the new audit techniques (Financial Status Auditing) that the IRS is trying to develop and pursue is to require that all agents spend more time interviewing taxpayers. They would spend enough time at the taxpayer's place of business and at the taxpayer's home to assess the mode of living and life style of each of the taxpayers being audited. This not only takes an inordinate amount of the agent's time, but it also puts many agents at risk of physical harm since they will be going into many businesses and homes that are dangerous. In the past, when the agent considered something dangerous, he could merely ask the taxpayer to come to the local IRS office for an audit. To protect the agents, the IRS must rethink this directive and find other means of getting the needed information.

Many of the new agents are not being trained in methods that will give the IRS the biggest bang for their bucks invested in the agent and the individual audits. It appears that most agents are being trained to think that all taxpayers are trying to beat the tax paying and collecting system and not to trust any taxpayer. Therefore, the agents are treating the taxpayer as a criminal suspect rather than a person who is helping pay the agent's salary. The new agents should be trained to be able to recognize what is important in a particular audit and what will give the IRS the most in additional taxes. Then, they should make these adjustments and move on to the next audit. This would give the service more audits with bigger assessments, and they could quit concerning themselves with the smaller audit adjustments that usually take more time and money to process than the agent collects. After the new agents are trained in the proper audit techniques, then their supervisors should be more responsive to helping them make proper decisions about what is important on each audit. This proper supervision should give each agent time to do twice the number of audits as they are doing at the present time. In the private sector, we realize the importance of proper training, proper planning, and proper supervision; and this must be followed by the service if they ever plan to do more audits that yield larger assessments.

Another area the IRS must address is that some of the audit agents, as well as the collection agents, are just plain rude to the taxpayers. We have all been taught that you can accomplish more by being polite than by being rude, and this should also be the case with the IRS. Even if a collection agent is going to have to take a piece of property from a taxpayer so that it can be sold for back taxes, the collection agent does not have to be rude and be-little the taxpayer. Most taxpayers that have this happen to them have already suffered some type of business failures or some large medical costs that have caused them to owe these back taxes. Therefore, the taxpayers are usually experiencing a feeling of low-esteem and even some guilt because of the conditions that they are facing. To prevent this rudeness, the service should have a calling card that each audit or collection agent presents to the taxpayer upon their initial contact. The card should give the agent's name and address, and the name and address of the agent's immediate supervisor. This calling card would instruct the taxpayer that they have the right to contact the supervisor if they believe that they are not being dealt with fairly or if they are being treated rudely. Once the agent's supervisor has been contacted by the taxpayer, the taxpayer should then be given in writing the name and address of this supervisor's immediate supervisor so the taxpayer can have someone else to contact if they still think that they are not being treated fairly.

If you have contacted one of the service centers to request any type of tax information, you know that it is almost impossible to get even a simple question answered. If you do receive an answer, many times it is incorrect. Since many taxpayers depend on these service centers to answer their questions, the IRS must solve this problem of their employees not being able to adequately answer these taxpayer questions. One of the solutions is for the IRS to hire as many tax professionals, as possible, during the peak filing season from January to April each year. These may be young mothers with accounting degrees who only want to work part-time while raising their families. Or they could hire retired professional accountants to fill these jobs. These employees would require very little training, and their answers would be accurate most of the time.

It must be remembered that some of the questions asked by the taxpayers can be very complex; therefore, the more experience the employee has, the more likelihood the question will be answered completely and correctly. To assist these employees on the more complex questions, the IRS must provide computer equipped CD-ROM readers. The employee can then find many areas on the computer by merely key stroking in key words about a subject. While the taxpayer is on the telephone, he can receive timely answers. If questions cannot be answered during the telephone call, the service center employee should be able to provide the answer by a return telephone call within a day or two. Better educated employees and the use of the high technical computer equipment should decrease the number of employees needed at the service center and give the taxpayer faster and more accurate answers to their questions.

The service centers are making many other errors, that proper management and supervision should be able to correct. The employees at these service centers apply many tax payments to the incorrect accounts, and it is then very difficult for the taxpayers to have corrections made. Many times IRS collection agents will call or come by your business to inquire about past due payments, only to find that all of your payments have been made and paid on a timely basis. This usually is very embarrassing to the taxpayer and helps to further alienate the taxpayers and the IRS.

Other errors that these service centers have made is to place the incorrect federal identification number on the deposit coupons or other forms that are mailed back to the taxpayer. The IRS keys in the federal identification numbers rather than the names of the taxpayers. If you use one of these incorrectly coded forms, it may take you months or even years to have your tax deposits or payments applied correctly to your account. It is suggested that you examine all documents coming from the IRS for correct name, address, and particularly correct federal identification or social security number.

In the past, we have all read about some of these service center employees shredding tax returns, so that they would not have to key them into the IRS computer system. We have also read about some of the employees surfing the IRS computer system to see how much some well-known person has made or to see what is reported on his return. If we as taxpayers insist that better management and supervision be practiced at the service centers and throughout the IRS, then most of these errors and other unacceptable practices will cease. The IRS management and supervision must make the employees more accountable for their work and performance.

If you have received a notice from the IRS recently, you have received a toll free number so that you can call them regarding any questions that you may have about the notice, or you can provide them with additional facts so that the questions on the notice can be resolved. If you tried to call this toll free number during any of 1995, you probably found that you got an answering machine or voice mail, and you were instructed to leave a message or to write to the IRS concerning the notice. If a message is left, it may take someone with IRS two to three weeks to get back in touch with you. Most tax professionals are advising their clients to write to the IRS rather than calling the toll free number so that the questions can be resolved much faster. The IRS is going to have to find ways to provide faster telephone and mail service.

For 1996, the IRS is providing the taxpayers with a new toll free number 1-800-829-8815. This new telephone number is being announced on IRS Notice 1035 and states “Need Help? Call Us Today!”. The notice advises taxpayers to call this NEW telephone number so that a Customer Service Representative can help you resolve your tax issues, and can provide you with a written response if necessary. Then, if only the last part of the notice is accurate; it states that “we are open to help you”. This service is supposed to operate from 8:00 A.M. to 11:00 P.M. Monday through Friday. Maybe using this new toll-free number and calling the IRS employee, a Customer Service Representative, will be a beginning in the right direction to provide the taxpayers the fast, friendly, and courteous service that we pay for with our hard earned tax dollars.

The IRS must work much closer with the tax professional and develop additional forms that these tax professionals can file electronically directly to each of the service centers. In recent years, more and more individual tax returns have been filed electronically with the IRS; however, all returns that the tax professionals are now preparing on their computer systems should be electronically filed directly from the tax professional's office to the IRS service centers. This would eliminate the need to re-input this computer data by service center employees once the hard copy is received by the IRS. Most corporate returns, partnership returns, fiduciary returns, information returns, and payroll reports could now be electronically filed directly with the service centers and reduce the need for many employees now used by these service centers. I believe that most tax professionals would be willing to work with the IRS in helping to streamline all facets of the direct electronic filing of the various forms as well as assisting the IRS in moving into more high-tech data processing.

The IRS must also work closer with the tax professional in closing audits. Just five years ago it was the agent complaining to the tax professional that audits were not being completed fast enough, and they usually blamed the tax professional if an audit was not completed in two to three months. But now it is the tax professional complaining to the IRS agents who are unable to close an audit in less than five or six months. Some of the simple audits that could be completed in one to two weeks are now taking some agents eleven and twelve months to complete. Again, IRS group managers and supervisors are going to have to work closer with the agents to help them make quicker decisions so that all facets of their work can flow through the system faster. If your audit seems to get bottlenecked, I suggest that you make weekly calls to the agent, and if the agent is not in the office, ask to speak to the group manager or supervisor. After two or three weeks they get tired of getting your weekly call and will sometimes get the paper-work moving again. The longer that you let the agent sit on the audit, the more audit adjustments he may be able to find.

Late in 1995, the IRS and the National Technical Information Service division of the Commerce Department announced that plans were being finalized to allow Internet users to electronically file their returns directly to FedWorld, which is the United States Internet on-line service. With the millions of home computers and taxpayers with on-line services, 30% to 40% of the tax returns could be filed electronically using this service. However, a large amount of fraud has been detected by the IRS from electronically filed returns in the past couple of years. I believe that by the IRS allowing everyone with a home computer to electronically file his return, they can expect much more fraud and abuse to occur, unless the IRS places the proper constraints on this new form of electronically filed returns.

In ten states, the IRS has been testing a pilot program called TeleFile. This is an attempt to produce alternative ways to file your returns. IRS Commissioner Margaret Milner Richardson said, “Filing taxes doesn’t get any easier than this.” For the 1995 returns that will be filed in 1996, rather than filing Form 1040EZ twenty three million taxpayers will be able to use their touch tone telephone to enter their tax data directly to the IRS computer system in about six minutes. This TeleFile program will compute your tax while you are on the telephone, and it will tell you the amount of your refund. You will even be given a confirmation number for tracking your return in case there is a problem. Those that will be eligible for this TeleFile filing must be single with no dependents, live at the same address as the prior year, have taxable income of less than $50,000, taxable interest income of $400 or less, and have no income from unemployment compensation. Since tax returns that are filed electronically contain fewer errors and are easier to process, you should consider using this TeleFile system if you qualify.

Another area that must be addressed by our elected officials is the estate and gift tax exemptions. The estate and gift tax exemption amounts to $600,000 for a taxpayer, and with proper tax planning, this can be increased to $1,200,000 for a taxpayer and the taxpayer's spouse. Therefore, there is very little incentive for anyone to accumulate any assets or wealth, as the federal and state estate taxes can be 50% or more when estates exceed these exemption amounts by $2,000,000. To give taxpayers more incentive to produce wealth, the estate and gift tax exemption amounts must be raised to an amount that will be double the current amount. This will probably need to be phased in over a two to five year period of time. The future exemption amounts will need to be indexed to inflation so the exemption amount will increase, and the taxpayer's estate will be taxed only for growth and not because of the increases created by inflation. Also, consideration must be given to having some type of discount on family businesses and farms when the estate is being valued for estate tax purposes. Usually the largest valued asset in an estate is the family business or farm, and these assets are very difficult to convert to cash so that the estate taxes can be paid.

The yearly gift tax amount that any taxpayer can give to

each recipient must also be increased from the current $10,000 amount to double this amount, and this will also probably need to be phased in over a two to five year period. The gift tax also needs to be indexed to inflation so that the amount will increase each year, and the taxpayers will be able to pass on gifts without inflation having such a negative effect.

Also, congress must make changes in the tax laws to be sure that all businesses are taxed the same. For instance, the depreciation rules for farmers should be changed so that the depreciation on farm machinery and equipment will be the same as on machinery and equipment in industry. This would permit the farmers to depreciate their assets using the 200 percent declining balance method rather than the current 150 percent declining balance method, and it would decrease the depreciation life on farm machinery and equipment from 10 years to 7 years. Since farming operations have been treading water for several years, this may help breathe some new life into them and possibly encourage others to begin farming businesses.

In 1992, the Section 179 depreciation deduction was increased from $10,000 to $17,500. This is taken the first year that the qualifying property is placed in service and is made on an item-by-item basis. This $17,500 must be increased to $35,000 or more so that businesses will have the option to write off assets faster. One of the few ways that our economy will continue to sustain growth is to encourage businesses to invest in new machinery and equipment by having the ability to write off some or all of the investment in the first year.

The deficit continues to increase each day because of the many social programs, and the United States is trying to police all of the countries of the world with our military. Therefore, congress must raise other funds if they are not going to raise our taxes. Some of the areas that congress should review as possible fund producers are to charge fees for admissions to all public parks and to the many federal buildings that have thousands of visitors each week. A review of all of the federal agencies and departments should be made to determine if any type of fees could be charged so that these agencies and departments can be self supporting. If only a few of these can become self supporting, then our deficit will disappear and our taxes will decrease considerably.

The United States economy for the past 10 to 12 years has been on an upswing and has had very low inflation during this period of time. Since what goes up must come down, we will probably see a different swing in the economy unless congress once again re-institutes the investment tax credit and the long term capital gain deduction that was eliminated in 1986. The investment tax credit provided for a 10% credit on qualified property that was purchased for a business or farm. This credit was used to reduce the federal income taxes dollar for dollar. For instance, if the taxpayer purchased a piece of equipment for $30,000, then a credit of $3,000 could be used to reduce income taxes.

The long term capital gain deduction for the years of 1982 through 1986 made the taxpayer have a maximum tax on these transactions of 20% of the total gain. During years since 1986, the tax on long term gains has varied, but since 1991 the tax rate has been 28% on the total gain. To keep the economy stimulated and to help create new jobs, these two areas must be reactivated. Then businesses will want to invest in new equipment, and taxpayers with venture capital will want to invest in new markets.

One other change is badly needed. When someone calls an IRS office or agent to report different types of tax evasion schemes, the IRS is going to have to be more responsive and do more investigation to determine if the information that they have received is correct. Of course, many calls are placed to the IRS because of envy and jealously of taxpayers. However, when the IRS receives several calls about the same evasion ploy, they should be able and willing to investigate.

We all hear much today from all of the various industries about downsizing, consolidating, outsizing, restructuring and modernizing. All federal, state, county and city governmental agencies must start making the same changes that are being made in the private sector. They need to be able to operate within the budgeted amount of tax dollars raised. To make sure that our elected officials take the necessary steps to make government run more as we do our businesses, we must try to elect more business oriented people to guide our government at all levels.

During the budget fight between congress and the President during the latter part of 1995, the IRS was notified to reduce their 115,000 employees. They were instructed to eliminate over 8,000 jobs through attrition, lay offs, and offering early retirement to employees until February 3, 1996. The IRS did not offer any early retirement incentives as has been the case with postal employees and TVA employees. It appears that many of the smaller IRS offices will be closed and consolidated with some of the larger offices. Hopefully this move will help to streamline the IRS and will not have any detrimental effect on the service to the taxpayers.

After the shutdown of the IRS and other governmental agencies during the middle of November 1995, and again during the middle of December 1995, the question has to be raised as to whether we need all of the current employees at the federal government level. We were told that approximately 800,000 employees were laid off in November 1995, and approximately 260,000 in December 1995. During these shutdowns, with no more inconveniences that we experienced, it may be a good time for our governing fathers to restructure some of the various governmental agencies. Where else could employees be laid off or fired for lack of funds and then be called back to work and told that they were going to be paid for the time off? This could only happen in the United States Government or because of United States politics.

The federal government has not balanced the yearly budget since Lyndon B. Johnson was president. If each of us exceeded our spending budget each year as much as is being done by our federal government, then not only would the government be bankrupt, but also would each of our family units. Late in October 1995, congress again stated that they planned to balance the budget in a seven year period of time.

Congress must balance the budget in a much shorter time frame than seven years. This means that each of us will have to bite the bullet by possibly paying more taxes and receiving less services from the government. Even the social programs are going to have to have some major changes if the budget is ever going to be balanced.

Congress has been running the economy on what they refer to as the four by four rule: one fourth of the cure takes place in four times the time. So if they tell us that something is going to be cured in one year, they expect the cure to be completed in a period of four years. Therefore, if they tell us that it is going to take seven years, then they expect that it is going to take four times longer, or twenty-eight years. Each of us is going to have to require our congressmen to have more fiscal responsibility than they are presently demonstrating.

Chapter 7

Estate Taxes: The IRS Gets You Coming and Going

AT THE PRESENT TIME, THE ESTATE AND gift tax exemption amounts to $600,000 for a taxpayer, (Congress is proposing to raise this exemption amount during a phase in period to $750,000) and with proper tax planning, this can be increased to $1,200,000 for a taxpayer and the taxpayer's spouse. After a taxpayer's assets have exceeded these amounts, the federal and state estate taxes can amount to 50% or more of the estate assets that exceed the exemption amounts by $2,000,000. When tax professionals meet with their clients, they explain that for each dollar increase in their estate assets they will not only be paying the regular income taxes while they are alive, but will be paying up to 50% or more of federal and state estate taxes upon the taxpayer's death. Most taxpayers state that they can see no reason to continue to accumulate wealth or assets if 50% or more is going to have to be paid in estate taxes upon their death. Also, most taxpayers will appear to be having heart failure when the tax professional tells them that this tax is due in 9 months after date of death. If the estate does not have enough cash available to pay the estate taxes, then some of the estate assets will have to be sold so that the estate taxes can be paid within the 9 month time frame.

If married, you must be sure that your attorney has provided the necessary provisions in both wills to give you and your spouse the maximum benefit so that both of the estates will be able to use the $600,000 estate and gift tax deduction or exclusion. Please do not assume that this is in your will, and please do not assume that your attorney will put these provisions in your will without your asking that it be included. I suggest that you spend the extra professional fees and ask your tax professional to review your will in rough draft form so that he will be able to make any recommendations concerning these or other provisions that may be overlooked by your attorney. Many attorneys will not ask enough questions when preparing a will, and many times they do not have any idea that a client's estate is above the exemption amount. Many taxpayers find out after a spouse has died that a simple provision in the deceased spouse's will would have given the couple twice the amount of exemption.

With the continual proposals made by congress in the estate and gift tax exemption deductions, it is important that your will provide for the maximum amount of exemption allowed at the time of death so that your will does not have to be changed each time the new proposals are enacted. For instance, congress is proposing that the exemption be raised to $750,000 with additional exemption amounts provided for businesses and farms. The provisions in your wills should provide for the maximum amount of these exemptions.

Many taxpayers have their wills prepared and then place

them in their lock boxes or leave them with their attorneys. The taxpayer then gives very little thought to these wills once they are prepared and filed away. Most tax professionals suggest that you review your will at least annually. Therefore, if you do place your original copy of your will in your lock box or leave it at your attorney's office, you should keep a copy. By placing your copy of the will in the front of your tax return folder at home or in your office, you will be reminded to review the provisions of your will each year while preparing your personal tax returns.

Some of the older taxpayers will tell their tax professionals that they do not need to prepare a will or do any estate tax planning because they have placed all of their properties, bank accounts, and stocks and bonds in joint accounts with right of survivorship with their children and grandchildren. These older taxpayers think that upon their death, these items will transfer to these recipients; therefore, estate taxes are eliminated.

When the older taxpayers are told that this type of transfer at their date of death does not eliminate the payment of estate taxes on these assets, most will either refuse to believe that this is correct or will completely ignore the tax professional's advice to do the necessary estate planning. If this is encountered by the tax professional, he should suggest to these older taxpayers to have their children or grandchildren meet with him and the taxpayer during any future tax planning sessions. If the children and grandchildren then understand that many dollars will be paid to the IRS in estate taxes upon the taxpayer's death, the tax professional will be better positioned to deal with these recipients of the estate assets. It will be much easier to explain why these recipients may have to pay up to 50% of the amounts that were jointly held by them in estate taxes.

These older taxpayers will also shock their tax professional by telling them that they have transferred a large amount of land, cash, or other assets to their children or grandchildren without any consideration that gift taxes are owed if the transfer exceeds the joint estate and gift exemption amount of $600,000. Many of these older taxpayers will tell this many months or many years after the transfer has taken place. This makes the filing of the gift tax return delinquent, and large penalties and interest are due on the returns when filed. Ignoring the fact that the return is supposed to be filed or ignorance of the gift tax laws does not prevent the IRS from collecting these gift taxes at a much later date.

Another problem that is created by transferring these assets by gift without consulting your tax advisor is that the tax basis transferred to the recipient is the same tax basis as that of the taxpayer. Therefore, besides owing gift taxes on the current market value of these assets, the recipient will have more income taxes to pay upon sale of these assets since they will have the taxpayer's lower tax basis in these assets. If the taxpayer waits until the date of death to let some of this low tax basis property pass to the recipient by will, then the recipient will have a stepped-up basis to the current market value. This will reduce the taxes the recipient will pay upon selling this property. It is very crucial that as much time as possible be spent with these older taxpayers and their children and grandchildren so that their estate, gift, and income taxes will be minimized.

Another problem encountered when doing estate tax planning is that many taxpayers want to do estate tax planning by removing assets from their estates, but the taxpayer does not want to give up complete control over these assets. Normally, if this control is not given up by the taxpayer, the IRS will bring these assets back into the taxpayer's estate as if no transfer had ever taken place.

Of course, to help reduce estate taxes once the exemption amount has been exceeded, the taxpayer should consider a continual gifting program to their children and grandchildren each year. These gifts can amount to $10,000 per recipient per year without any gift tax being due or without reducing the joint estate and gift tax exemption amount. Many times the taxpayer and his spouse overlook the provision of making a joint gift to each recipient of $20,000 per year. This can be done by the taxpayer and the spouse each transferring $10,000 per recipient or by noting on the check or other gifting document that it is the intent of the taxpayer and the spouse that the gift be a joint gift, and both the taxpayer and spouse sign the check or other gifting document. Most tax advisors recommend that gift tax returns be prepared on these yearly gift amounts. This gives notice to the IRS that you have assigned a certain market value to the items being gifted. After the three year statute of limitation has run, and after filing these returns, it is usually difficult for the IRS to come in and challenge your values, unless you have grossly understated these values.

The IRS is most likely to take a long and hard look at the transfers involving closely held businesses and corporations that have been transferred at a big discount because the taxpayer holds a minority interest in them. Many times these large discounted minority ownership interest amounts can be justified either to the IRS agent or to IRS appeals and should be aggressively pursued when using these for gifting purposes. Always be sure that your tax advisor maintains and agrees with the method that you are using in arriving at these discounted values. Then, he will be in a position to convince an IRS agent of the values you are using should your gift tax returns be audited.

When doing your planned gifting for federal gift tax purposes, be sure to remember that most states also have gift taxes, and some of the states do not have the same rules and regulations as the IRS; therefore, your planned giving must also conform to your individual state of residence. Also, most states require that state gift tax returns be filed if a return is filed for federal purposes.

Estate taxes are due nine months after the date of death, and most estates do not have enough cash to pay all of the federal and state estate taxes and estate administration fees. Therefore, provisions should be made by the taxpayer to insure that his estate will have enough cash to pay the related taxes and fees without the executor having to sell assets to raise the necessary cash for paying these taxes and fees.

A method that many are using to provide the necessary cash to pay these estate taxes and administration fees is through life insurance trusts. The taxpayer sets up a life insurance trust with the proceeds of the life insurance payable to the children or grandchildren upon his death. Since the insurance is in the life insurance trust, and the proceeds are payable to the children or grandchildren upon death, the insurance proceeds are not includable in the estate and are not subject to estate taxes. The premium payments for this life insurance are treated as gifts to the children or grandchildren each year. Therefore, it may reduce the amount of other gifts that you may be able to give because of the $10,000 gift tax limitation. Since the largest amount of estate taxes and administration fees are due upon the death of the second spouse, many taxpayers and their spouses are obtaining second to die life policies for these insurance trusts. These second to die policies are usually less expensive than other life policies and can usually be written even when one of the spouses has been rejected for an individual life policy because of medical or other problems such as alcoholism or mental conditions.

In many estates, the life insurance proceeds will make up the majority of the estate, and because of these life insurance proceeds, the estate will have to pay federal and state estate taxes. If you make your spouse, children, or grandchildren the owners and beneficiaries of your life insurance policies, then these life insurance proceeds will not be includable in your estate. Of course, there can be negative points to consider when structuring your life insurance policies like this. There could be a divorce or a child or grandchild who is a spend thrift who would be able to cash in the life policies since they are the owners.

Even though the estate tax return is due nine months after date of death, how long should I leave an estate open? Most attorneys and tax professionals will recommend that you close an estate as soon as practical. By leaving an estate open longer, more administration fees and expenses will have to be paid. Also, an estate must file and pay an income tax for all income made while the estate is open. The income tax rate for an estate is 39.6% for all taxable income over $7,650. Many times by closing an estate, this income can be shifted to a taxpayer whose tax rate is lower than this rate. If an estate has income of over $600, then an income tax return must to be filed. The estate taxable income is like that for a trust tax return; both begin paying taxes at a small amount of income and then will begin paying the maximum amount of tax on taxable income over $7,650. Of course, if an estate is under $600,000, no federal estate tax return is due. However, if these estates have income of $600 or more before they are closed, then an income tax return is due to be filed.

When doing estate planning, the taxpayer often will ask if different types of trusts will help to reduce some of the estate taxes. Many times your tax professional or attorney will help in setting up trusts that are needed while you are still alive as well as trusts that are needed for estate purposes after you are deceased. One of the things that is often overlooked when setting up these trusts is that if the trust is not set up where the income is passed through and taxed to a recipient, then the trust usually has a much higher rate of tax to pay than does the recipients. As previously stated, during 1995 the federal income tax rate for trust returns was 39.6% for all income over $7,650. Of course, state income taxes of at least 5% are also generally due on this taxable income. Be sure that your attorney prepares all trusts where the income will be taxed to the beneficiaries if these beneficiaries are being taxed in a lower tax bracket.

One of the trusts that is becoming more poplar in estate tax planning is the Living Trust. This helps your estate to avoid probate and the related court costs, and it provides more flexibility and privacy in settling your estate.

In doing estate planning, taxpayers often overlook the Living Will. This Living Will generally provides your medical doctor or hospital with your wishes concerning when you want life support treatment to be applied and when you want it to be withheld. If this document is not in place, your estate may end up paying thousands of dollars of medical bills that you never wanted to occur. You may desire not to be connected to life support systems that can keep you hanging on for weeks or even months.

Power of attorney should also be considered when you are doing your estate tax planning. These documents allow the person or persons that you name in this document to carry on your business affairs should you become physically or mentally incapacitated. There are different types of power of attorneys, and your attorney should be able to help you to tailor your document to fit your individual needs.

Since the IRS gets you coming and going, you can do just a little estate planning each year, and this will help you alleviate thousands of dollars of taxes for your estate to pay.

Chapter 8

How Much Tax is Too Much Tax?

THIS QUESTION HAS EVIDENTLY BEEN ASKED FOR many years. We read in the Good Book in Luke 2:1-5 that King Augustus decided to tax ALL the world. Joseph and Mary had to go to Bethlehem to pay their taxes and had the Savior of the world while there. In Matthew 22:21, we are not told how much tax we should pay; however, we are encouraged to pay taxes due to our governments. Throughout this Good Book we read about the Publicans who were the tax collectors, and most hated by their countrymen, because they usually exhorted or collected too much tax. In Matthew 9, we read about Saint Matthew and in Luke 19, we read about Zacchaeus who were probably two of the few honest tax collectors during this period.

When you ask 10 taxpayers the question of how much tax is too much tax, you will probably receive 10 different answers. The answers will probably range from no tax, to as much as 35% tax. I have asked many people this question, and it appears that most people only think about the federal income tax portion of our tax burden and do not give much consideration to our large amount of social security tax, medicare tax, or our state tax burden.

Most taxpayers pay at least 15% federal income taxes. Social security and medicare taxes are 7.65%, and state income taxes are generally at least 5%. To these amounts another 7.65% of social security and medicare taxes and approximately 3% state unemployment taxes are paid by the employer. Of course, each of us pays 5% to 10% state and local sales tax on each consumer item and food product that we purchase each day. Then, as if these were not a large enough tax burden for each of us, we have to pay higher and higher real estate taxes on our homes and businesses each year. Please do not forget the taxes that we pay for our car tags, car inspection stickers, business license; and the list go on and on. After adding all of the different types of taxes that we pay, the total tax burden is probably 40% to 70% for most of us.

Each year around May 15 is considered "tax freedom day" because the money earned from January through the middle of May simply pays our taxes for the year. However, if you include each taxpayer's portion of the yearly federal deficit and the other regulatory costs, "tax freedom day" would actually end up in the middle of July.

Most of us realize that the only way the federal government and the state and local governments can operate and carry on their normal every day functions of providing highway and road systems, police and fire protection, and other governmental services is by our payment of taxes into these systems. When thinking of the services, we often forget that most of our tax dollars are paid by these governmental agencies for interest and debt service, and for many social programs and services for those that are not working and contributing to the tax system. Even though most of us believe that we are compelled or obligated to pay taxes, we will often make the statement that we want to pay our fair share, or that we want to pay what we owe, but we do not want to pay one dollar more. Most of us also state that we would not mind paying our taxes or even more taxes, if our governmental agencies would spend the tax money more wisely and would spend within the budgeted amount of taxes collected as our families have to budget based on our family income.

Other reasons that many of us do not want to pay taxes are the waste, fraud, and inefficiencies that exist within our government programs and social programs. Many taxpayers state that if foreign aid were eliminated they would not oppose paying taxes as much as they do. However, only 1% of the current budget is being used for foreign aid, and 50% of this amount is being sent to Israel and Egypt.

How much tax is too much tax? Most of us will agree that it is going to take our governmental entities more than 25% of our income in taxes to function properly, and most of us will also agree that we should not be expected to pay more than 40% to 45% of our total income on any and all type of taxes, including sales tax. If our federal income taxes amounted to 15% to 20% of our income, and our social security and medicare taxes amounted to the present combined rate of 15.3%, then other federal or state and local taxes amounting to 10% to 15% should be an amount that all governmental agencies should be able to operate on adequately.

One industry that appears to be paying more than its fair

share of taxes is the trucking industry. With the exorbitant taxes and tremendous paper work, it is a wonder that so many taxpayers try to make a living in this business. These businesses pay a federal highway-use tax on Form 2290 of generally $550 per unit. They also pay a fuel tax in every state based on the miles driven at $.17 to $.25 per gallon of diesel fuel. To calculate this fuel tax an International Fuel Tax Agreement (IFTA) report has to be filed quarterly. All southeastern states other than Kentucky are covered by this reporting form. A federal excise tax of approximately 10% is due on the purchase of the trucks and trailers. The apportioned state tags for the trucks cost about $1,500 per year, and the trailer tags usually cost between $250 and $300. Of course, there are sales taxes that have to be paid on these units when they are purchased. Then, there are the usual payroll and other taxes paid by all businesses. These businesses have to comply with ICC and federal and state DOT rules, regulations, and report requirements. Then the regulatory cost of special insurance, special driver licenses, employee physicals, state fuel bonds, and single state registration fees must be added.

Who is paying the most in income taxes? In 1983, the top 1% ranked by income was paying little more than 20% of the federal taxes. By 1993, this top 1% of the taxpayers was paying 30% of the federal taxes. Also, those taxpayers earning 50% or less ranked by income was paying 7% of the federal taxes. In 1993, this same group of taxpayers paid less than 5% of the federal taxes. This tells us that the average taxpayer was paying the majority of the federal income taxes in 1983 and in 1993. Even with continued changes in the tax laws, the average American taxpayer is going to have to carry the tax load so that our large government bureaucracy can keep the social programs and big government going.

We all should be quick to tell our congressmen and other government leaders how much tax is too much tax. We often hear our congressmen give the quote of "don't tax you, don't tax me, but tax that man behind the tree." However, with the new tax laws that are passed from time to time, it appears that most of us are the "man behind the tree."

There have to be thousands of quotable quotes that each of us have read or heard over the years concerning government and taxes; however, a quote from William E. Borah in a speech to the United States Senate probably is one of the best. "The marvel of all history is the patience with which men and women submit to burdens unnecessarily laid upon them by their governments."

Even with our growing budget deficit, congress decided to reduce our taxes late in 1995, thereby telling each of us that we have been paying too much in taxes. The new tax law is called the 1995 Revenue Reconciliation Act and is the biggest tax law change in ten years. The proposed changes in this tax bill will once again give individuals the benefits of capital gains, new types of IRAs, changes in the alternative minimum tax, increase in estate exemptions, changes in 401K contributions for highly compensated employees, and a family tax credit. It will also extend the expiring tax credits for targeted jobs credit and the tax credits for research and development expenses.

On October 26, 1995, congress passed the Balanced Reconciliation Act of 1995 giving a tax cut of $354 billion. On October 27, 1995, the senate passed the Omnibus Budget Reconciliation Act giving a tax cut of $245 billion. These tax reductions were never passed into law, and many representatives and senators believe that the actual tax cut will be approximately $150 billion to $170 billion. With our growing budget deficit, due to the cost of our social programs and the payment of interest on the national debt, I believe that a $50 billion to $75 billion tax reduction would be more realistic.

Of the $245 billion tax reduction being proposed by the house of representatives, one-half is attributable to the family tax credit which provides $500 per child tax credit.

All of us agree that we pay too much in taxes; however, congress must act responsibly when enacting large tax cuts that cannot possibly be offset by reduced government spending.

Chapter 9

IRS New Audit Procedures - (We Will Get You One Way or the Other)

YOU THINK THAT YOU HAVE MASTERED ALL of the audit procedures and techniques of the IRS, and then they come along with a few new surprises for the taxpayers and the tax professionals. The new buzz words being used by those in the IRS are "Market Segment Specialization Program," audit techniques guides, "Financial Status Auditing," and "Compliance 2000".

The "Compliance 2000" program was begun by the IRS due to criticism from the United States General Accounting Office. They insisted that efforts and techniques must be developed by the IRS to find ways to detect unreported and under reported income on corporation and business Schedule Cs for individual taxpayers. Within this "Compliance 2000" program, the IRS has developed the "Financial Status Auditing" program (previously known as "Economic Reality Auditing").

The "Financial Status Auditing" program will attempt to develop an economic profile of the individual taxpayer by using the conventional auditing procedures and by looking at the complete lifestyle of the taxpayer. Most tax professionals believe that the decision by the IRS to audit a return using this new audit program indicates that the agent intends to find adjustments on each return selected, to yield additional taxes to be collected. Many of the questions being asked by the agent and the methods being used by the agents to obtain information, resemble the questions and methods that are used by the criminal investigation division agents. Therefore, many tax professionals are asking these agents if their clients are being investigated for criminal proceedings or if the audit is just a routine audit.

Many of the agents are demanding more and more questions be answered about the taxpayer's lifestyle and other personal habits of the taxpayer and the taxpayer's family. This procedure makes having your tax professional present during your initial meeting with the IRS agent very essential. The Taxpayer Bill of Rights gives the taxpayer the right to representation during an examination or interview with the IRS agent. Do not let an agent attempt to persuade you that your tax professional is not needed for your interview or your audit. Many taxpayers are finding that the agents are telling them that they want to come by their house or business to ask a few questions or obtain some additional information. When asked by the taxpayer if the tax professional is also coming, the agents are telling the taxpayer that it will only take a few minutes, and the tax professional is not needed during this meeting. If this happens during your audit, you should refuse to meet with or talk with the agent without your tax professional present.

The IRS is now steadily preparing new Market Segment Specialization Program audit technique guides. These will direct the IRS agent when conducting audits in a specialized field. These audit guides provide information for the agent to follow when doing their audits and help them to make decisions as to whether a certain taxpayer in a particular business may be under reporting income or overstating expenses. These guides give details that the agents will be following to do future audits and can and should be obtained by the taxpayer for their related field of work. At the present time these are the 21 different audit guides:

-Air Charters
-Architects
-Attorneys
-Auto Body and Repair Industry
-Bars and Restaurants
-Beauty and Barber Shops
-Bed and Breakfasts
-Entertainment : Foreign Athletes and Entertainers
-Entertainment Industry - Music Industry
-Gas Retailers
-Ministers
-Mobile Food Vendors
-Mortuaries
-Music Industry
-Passive Activity Losses
-Reforestation Industry
-Rehabilitation Tax Credit
-Resolution Trust Corporation - Debt Cancellation
-Taxicabs
-Trucking Industry
-Wine Industry

You may obtain these audit guides by requesting the guide by name from IRS, Freedom of Information Reading Room, P. O. Box 795, Ben Franklin Station, Washington, DC 20044. The cost of the audit guides vary in price; however, the IRS gives you a $15.00 credit on your initial order request, and all but three audit guides are less than this amount. The Mortuaries audit guide is $22.80, the Passive Activity Losses guide is $27.90, and the Trucking guide is $17.10. You would owe the IRS the difference between these amounts and the $15.00 credit. If you want to order several of these guides, you may want to consider having some of your friends to each order a guide so that there will be no charges.

If your business is included in the 21 audit guides listed, you are encouraged to get a copy so that you can become familiar with all of the procedures and techniques that the IRS will be using against you during an audit on your company.

You may think that the IRS has overlooked your business or industry since your particular business is not listed. Be patient; the IRS is churning out a new guide for other market segments every month or two. As quick as the IRS comes out with an audit guide for your business, be sure to order one immediately. Then you can begin to prepare for the day that you will receive your IRS audit notice.

The Taxpayer Compliance Measurement Program (TCMP) fact sheet has recently been mailed to all IRS agents. It states that the agent is to place heavy emphasis on the "economic reality" of the tax return data being examined. The fact sheet also states that the scope of the audit will cover all return line items and that intensive indirect methods, cash t-accounts and other regular audit procedures will be used to ensure correct income reporting. The TCMP cases are to be assigned to agents that are considered specialists in a particular market segment.

At least two IRS service centers have again stated that the taxpayer can decline answering questions asked by the IRS agents during "economic reality" audits. An IRS newsletter for tax practitioners presented an article on economic reality audits that stated: "...a taxpayer does not have to answer an agent's questions. This includes those being asked to determine moneys expended for personal assets and support. In this situation, agents will arrive at a determination based on the records provided by the taxpayer." The article also states that the chief compliance officer with the IRS is meeting with professional organizations to get input as to the proper manner that the IRS can present economic reality auditing techniques and tools to the taxpayer.

These TCMP audits are supposed to cover 1994 tax returns that are filed with the IRS during 1995. This TCMP audit cycle was scheduled to begin in October 1995, and is expected to be completed by March 1998. The random sampling of these TCMP audits will be for 153,000 returns and will cover 4 types of returns. The breakdown of returns being audited are as follows:

TYPES OF RETURN	PRIOR TCMP	CURRENT TCMP
Form 1040	56,000	92,000
Form 1120	19,000	36,000
Form 1065	27,000	12,500
Form 1120S	10,000	12,500
	112,000	153,000

In late October 1995, the IRS announced that they were going to completely eliminate the above TCMP audits and that they were going to quit doing random auditing of tax returns. The IRS has stated this indefinite postponement of the TCMP audits was due to the congressional budget cuts, and they are now looking for other methods to gather the information that had been obtained by these audits.

Many tax professionals believe that if the IRS does in fact eliminate these TCMP audits, the DIF scoring technique that has long been the method used to detect unreported or under reported income by the IRS will be severely compromised. When the IRS realizes that they have made the wrong decision in a year or two, it will take them eight to ten years to recover from this postponing or eliminating these TCMP audits. Also, the fact that random sampling of tax returns will not be done encourages those that may cheat on their returns to open the flood gates and have little fear that the IRS will catch them if they file false or fraudulent tax returns.

With these new developments, it is very important that the IRS take a closer look at the Value Added Tax or some other method of assessing and collecting taxes so that further eroding of the our tax system will not occur.

Chapter 10

How to Audit Proof Your Returns

WHEN WE FILE OUR RETURNS EACH YEAR, we often wonder what can be done to keep the IRS from "pulling" our return for audit or review. Many times classifying our expenses a certain way on our business or farm schedule or knowing what to and what not to include on our itemized deductions may help to audit proof our tax returns.

Most taxpayers have thought that filing extensions and extending their tax returns from April 15 to August 15 was a good way to have the IRS audit or review their returns. However, in recent years it has been determined that filing these extensions and the return late, somehow short-circuits the IRS in picking these returns for audit. Many of the extended returns are being passed by and other returns being selected. I do not suggest that you necessarily extend your returns as the IRS is becoming more aware of the extended returns being overlooked for audit and review purposes and will probably be attempting to pick more of these returns in the future.

Another consideration of which you should be aware before you extend your returns is that by extending your returns you are giving the IRS additional time to audit your returns. The statute of limitation is extended for the same amount of time that your return is being extended. The automatic extension from April 15 to August 15, therefore, extends your statue of limitation on the return for 4 months. If you write the IRS to request that your return be extended from August 15 to October 15, the statute of limitation is extended another 2 months. If there is anything on your return that you believe may give you some auditing trouble, you may not want the statute of limitation to be extended past the normal 3 year statute of limitation. Of course, if there is anything on your return that is of a fraudulent nature, then the statute of limitation never runs out.

If I have my returns electronically filed, am I more likely or less likely to be audited? Since returns have only been being filed for a few years electronically, there is no definite answer to this question; however, it appears that fewer electronically filed returns are being audited than returns that are being mailed to the IRS service centers.

If I have a tax professional to prepare my returns, is it less likely that I will be audited? Throughout the United States, the IRS will audit approximately 1% to 5% of all types of returns being filed, and most tax professionals experience a smaller percentage of their returns being picked for audit purposes than the national average. This smaller percentage can be attributed to several things, but probably the most important factor is that the tax professionals have fewer mistakes on their returns since most of them use excellent computer packages in doing their client's tax returns. Also the experienced personnel on the tax professional's staff can help to classify your expenses on your particular schedules and help to prevent an audit of your return.

What are some of the things that the IRS will be looking at on my return that may cause it to be "pulled" for audit? On your Schedule A itemized deductions, the IRS will usually audit your return if you have unusually high contribution deductions and especially large amounts of non-cash contributions such as clothes, computer equipment, and other personal property.

Another item on Schedule A that will usually get your return checked is large casualty loss deductions. These casualty losses are usually from losses sustained from automobile wrecks or from fires where you do not have adequate insurance to pay for all of the economic loss sustained. In recent years, there have also been large casualty losses suffered by taxpayers from earthquakes, ice storms, and floods. Since the casualty loss deduction is generally limited to the amount of the tax basis not covered by insurance and is further reduced by 10% of adjusted gross income, most taxpayers will have to sustain a sizable casualty loss before any of the amount will be deductible.

Still another item on Schedule A that is getting many returns audited is the mortgage interest deduction on the personal residence. Many times the mortgage interest deduction is shown correctly on the taxpayer's tax return; however, the amount that the mortgage company reports to the IRS on Form 1098 may show an incorrect amount or may show the incorrect social security number. Or the mortgage company in some cases just fails to send these forms to the IRS. Another problem that the IRS has experienced in recent years on these Forms 1098 is that after they have received the correct forms from the mortgage company, the IRS has coded these into their computer system as interest income rather than interest expense. This creates a nightmare for the taxpayer and the tax professional to try and get corrected.

Another item that the IRS has been auditing very extensively in the last couple of years is contract labor. The IRS has developed a set of twenty questions that they have been applying to contract labor. If the taxpayer does not answer the twenty questions to their satisfaction, the IRS will reclassify the contract labor amounts to employee salaries. This usually means that the taxpayer will owe many thousand dollars of employment taxes. Trucking companies, building contractors, and other businesses in the contract selling business have especially been assessed large sums for employment taxes. In many cases they have been closed because they have been unable to pay the taxes that have been assessed for generally a three year period. Before agreeing to pay these employment taxes, you should exhaust all appeal rights that your CPA thinks are appropriate. This is especially important if you have been audited by the IRS in past years and no adjustments were made or suggested by a prior IRS agent during the audit.

For the 1994 returns, another item that has probably had many returns reviewed or checked is the earned income credit for taxpayers with a child, and with relatively low income. It appears that this particular credit has cost the government billions of dollars of abuse from taxpayers willing to do whatever is necessary to claim this credit. Since this is a negative income tax and pays these taxpayers back more than they have paid in taxes, the IRS holding back these refunds has caused many low income taxpayers a financial strain during 1995. These taxpayers had routinely received these amounts in prior years and had set their spending habits accordingly. It appears that fewer of these returns were reviewed or checked if tax professionals prepared the return.

There are other items that can make the IRS examine and "pull" your return for audit. Some are office at-home expense deductions, travel and entertainment expense deductions, and Schedule Cs and Schedule Fs with large losses. They may also examine your return when you are claiming an exemption other than for a dependent child, or large passive loss deductions on low income housing claimed on Schedule E. Three way swap transactions, a business whose gross profit percentage appears unusually low, or a business whose expenses appear unusually high also draw attention. Sometimes they notice a business with large vehicle expense deductions, a business that appears to have too many vehicles on the depreciation schedule, debt cancellation, or a combination of several of these items. The more of these items appearing on your tax return, the higher the DIF score will be for your tax return. The higher the DIF score is the more likely that your return will be "pulled" for audit.

Your tax professional will be able to help you slot these items on your returns to give you less probability of being audited. The tax professional will sometimes encourage you not to use or include some items on your return, since the time, expense, and hassle of an audit does not justify the tax savings of including some items on your return.

You may have been filing your own return and find that you have an unusual transaction that you do not feel comfortable placing on your return. You should seek out help from a tax professional on this transaction or in preparing your return for at least a year.

If you prepare your tax return each year, you can help audit proof your return by purchasing one of the computer tax programs on the market. These tax programs usually cost between $30.00 and $50.00. They help to assure you that your tax return is mathematically correct and help you to slot your data in the correct place. You can also purchase state tax packages with most of these new tax packages, and many of the programs allow you to print your federal and state forms on dot matrix or laser printers.

Also, if you prepare you tax return and have any type of business Schedule C, farm Schedule F, or other type of forms to complete, you should consider obtaining a reference book such a CCH or RIA. These books give information on most all type forms and filing requirements. Another service that I suggest is the Income Tax & Financial Planning Quickfinder Handbook from TMI Tax Services, Inc., 14700 Excelsior Boulevard, Minnetonka, MN 55345. This company also has a Small Business Quickfinder Handbook that is very helpful for questions with partnerships, corporations and fiduciaries and estates. Their telephone number is (612)935-6111 and their Fax number is (612)935-6121.

If you complete your own returns, you should order IRS Publication 17 Your Federal Income Tax for Individuals, and Publication 334 Tax Guide for Small Business. Many of your filing questions can be answered quickly in these publications, and for questions that cannot be found in these publications, you will find references for other IRS publications that will usually answer most of your questions.

After buying, reading, and studying the computer programs and reference books, you will probably find that you actually spend less money by just hiring a tax professional to prepare your return. You will certainly save much time and anxiety by using the professional service.

There are some common errors that may delay your refund, result in your receiving IRS notices, or cause your returns to be reviewed or checked. Most of these errors result from the following:

(A) earned income credit calculated incorrectly if your income is relatively low and a child lived with you;

(B) math errors through-out your return, but especially if you have taxable social security benefits;

(C) not checking your math and all tax computations several times;

(D) not checking all of the appropriate boxes on page 2 of Form 1040 for standard or itemized deductions, and the appropriate boxes for age 65 or older or for blindness;

(E) not placing your name, address, and social security numbers on all forms and checked for correctness;

(F) not attaching all required Forms W-2 and Forms 1099 if there is any income tax withheld;

(G) not signing and dating your return; and

(H) not writing your social security number on your check if a balance is due.

If you have a question about your return and do not want to talk with an IRS employee, you can call the IRS Tele-Tax number to find out about 150 different recorded topics. This same number is used to check the status of your refund. There are local numbers provided for the larger cities for this Tele-Tax service. For other areas and locations, you may use 1-800-829-4477 to obtain this information.

Chapter 11

Don't Stack Me with Taxes

AFTER WE HAVE FILED OUR RETURNS AND paid all of the taxes that we thought were due, we, as an individual taxpayer, may get a notice from the IRS stating that we owe additional tax for Alternative Minimum Tax. Our corporation may receive a notice that we owe this same Alternative Minimum Tax, Accumulated Earnings Tax, or Personal Holding Company taxes.

Many of us have not heard of these taxes, and we find that they stack on top of the huge amount of taxes that we have previously paid. We may get "heartlock" when we see the large amount of assessments that we get from the IRS. When meeting with your professional tax advisor, you should ask if there is a possibility that any of these taxes apply to your personal or corporate tax returns. If any of them do apply, your tax advisor may be able to help you do your tax planning so that you will not be surprised with an assessment in a year or so from the IRS.

Because of the type of taxes discussed in this chapter, some of the information is technical; however, I wanted to make you aware of these taxes. I believe that I have presented enough information to help you decide if you or your corporation are subject to these taxes.

Alternative Minimum Tax

The Alternative Minimum Tax (AMT), as previously stated, is in addition to your regular tax and was set up by congress to help assure that taxpayers who have too many tax deductions and pay very little in taxes, will at least pay a certain minimum amount. This tax is supposed to provide some tax equity to taxpayers who are not able to use large deductions and exemptions. This is a case where the taxpayer is given a tax deduction or benefit, and then has some or all of the deduction or benefit removed because of this tax. When you are doing your tax planning with your tax professional, you may be able to postpone deductions or accelerate some income so that you will not be liable for this tax. The additional tax for individual taxpayers is 26% of your first $175,000 of alternative minimum taxable income (AMTI), which is in excess of the exemption amount and 28% of any additional AMTI. It is calculated on Form 6251. For corporations, the AMT is 20% of the excess alternative minimum taxable income over their AMTI exemption amount, and it is calculated on Form 4626. The AMTI is the primary figure that has to be determined in figuring the excess tax saved by the deductions that the taxpayer has taken.

The exemption amount for married taxpayers filing a joint return is $45,000. This amount is reduced by 25% of the amount that AMTI exceeds $150,000, and it is therefore completely phased out when AMTI equals $330,000. This exemption amount is $33,750 for single taxpayers, and is $22,500 for married taxpayers filing separate returns, and for estates and trusts. The exemption amount for corporations is $40,000.

In calculating the AMTI, you generally begin with the regular taxable income and increase this amount by items known as tax preference items (TPIs). These TPIs are generally the items on your tax return that have reduced your tax to the amount that allows the AMT to kick in, and then you have to pay this tax in addition to your regular tax.

The adjustments and preference items that are added back to your taxable income include some of the itemized deductions on Schedule A. Medical and dental expenses are increased to 10% of adjusted gross income. The miscellaneous itemized deductions that exceed 2% of AGI, and the payment of state and local taxes are all added back to taxable income in arriving at AMTI. Also, there is no deduction for personal exemptions, and the standard deduction can not be claimed for AMTI.

Other items that may effect and increase AMTI is investment interest expense, accelerated depreciation, passive activities, tax-exempt interest from private activity bonds issued after August 7, 1986, charitable contributions, installment sales, intangible drilling costs, research and experimental costs, and tax shelter farm activities. Just in case the IRS has missed anything, there is an item listed for related adjustments. Besides those listed, there are approximately seven other items on Form 6251; however, these seven items would probably apply to very few taxpayers. The adjustments and tax preference items for corporations in arriving at AMTI are basically the same type items that appear on the individual taxpayer's return. On the corporate Form 4626, there is also an item listed by the IRS as other adjustments. This appears just in case they have missed anything on the corporate returns.

If you prepare your personal return or your corporate return, be sure to obtain the instructions for these forms. The instructions for these forms on the personal return are approximately 19 pages, and the instructions for these forms on the corporate return are approximately 20 pages. It always amazes and amuses me that it takes so many pages of instructions to explain just one form that the IRS expects the taxpayer to be able to complete, when most taxpayers have only a basic knowledge of these forms and tax laws. With the number of pages of instructions for these forms, the tax professionals sometimes have a hard time agreeing on the exact amount that should be slotted on each line of the forms.

If the IRS does adjust your return at the service center or by an audit for this AMT, be sure to review the details of the adjustment with a tax professional before you agree with the adjustment. Many of the agents are unable to accurately calculate this tax, even when they are using their lap top computers, and it often helps to question every item that an agent adjusts because of the complexity of the forms and the instructions.

Accumulated Earnings Tax

The corporate accumulated earnings tax is 39.6% of the improperly accumulated taxable income for the tax year. This tax is in addition to the regular tax of the corporation. This tax is actually a penalty that is imposed against a corporation for allowing its earnings to be accumulated rather than being distributed to and taxed to the individual shareholders. For the corporation to be subject to this tax, there must be an intended tax avoidance motive to avoid the income being passed on and taxed to its shareholders. When the corporation accumulates income in excess of its business needs, the IRS will generally say that this is a tax avoidance motive and will assess the corporation accordingly.

The accumulated taxable income is the taxable income of the corporation which is adjusted for (a) deduction for federal income taxes; (b) deduction for unlimited charitable contributions; (c) no deduction for net operating losses; (d) deduction for adjusted net current capital losses; (e) deduction for adjusted net current capital gains; and (f) no deduction for capital loss carry back or carry over. The taxable income is also reduced by the dividends paid deduction and the accumulated earnings credit.

The accumulated earnings credit amounts to $250,000, and it can be from past and present earnings of the corporation. For personal service corporations, this accumulated earnings credit is $150,000; however, since the income on these personal service corporations is regularly taxed at 35% each year, it is very uncommon to have any large amount of income left to accumulate. In controlled groups of corporations, there is only one

$250,000 of accumulated earnings credit permitted, and publicly held corporations with many shareholders are also subject to the tax.

Investment or holding companies that basically have assets composed of cash, stocks, bonds and other types of investments can use the $250,000 accumulated earnings credit only before the tax is imposed.

If the accumulated income of a corporation begins to exceed the accumulated earnings credit, then the corporation must be ready to justify the reasonable business needs of these excess accumulated earnings. Since the statute does not tell us what reasonable business needs are, there are acceptable and unacceptable reasons listed in the regulations. The acceptable grounds are (a) business expansion and plant replacement; (b) acquisition of a business through purchase of stock or assets; (c) debt retirement; (d) working capital; (e) necessary investments or loans to suppliers or customers for the maintenance of the corporate business; and (f) a reasonable amount of self-insurance for product liability risks. The unacceptable grounds listed in the regulations are (a) loans to shareholders and payments for their personal benefits; (b) loans to relatives or friends of shareholders or to others with no reasonable connection to the business; (c) loans to a controlled corporation; (d) investments that are not business related; and (e) accumulations for unrealistic risks or hazards.

Stock redemption to pay estate taxes and expenses is usually a good cause to accumulate income. Also, another good cause to accumulate income is the redemption of a minority interest of stock to prevent dissent and prevent the minority interest from being acquired by someone hostile to the corporation. The redemption of the majority interest of stock in a corporation is not usually a good reason to accumulate income.

In cases of excess accumulated income, the burden of proof usually falls to the corporation. In tax court cases on this issue, there are two instances where the burden of proof falls to the government. These deal with proper notification to the corporation. After proper notification, the corporation responds within 60 days with a statement providing reasonable grounds for these accumulated earnings.

A corporation is allowed operating expenses such as purchasing inventory, increasing of accounts receivable, or for expanding the plant. However, if your corporation has a large amount of cash that is not required to carry on normal operations, then you will possibly be assessed with this accumulated earnings tax if the IRS audits your corporation. If you plan to expand your business over the next three to five years and are going to need these accumulated earnings to purchase inventory, to purchase machinery and equipment, or for plant expansion, you might want to note this in the corporate minutes to establish a reasonable need for these accumulated earnings. Of course, after this period of time has passed and your corporation has not started to make plans to begin any of this expansion, you may be assessed for this tax by the IRS if your corporation is audited.

If your corporation is assessed for this tax, it could be for up to a three year period and could be substantial. Also, there will be a considerable amount that will be added for interest and possibly a penalty for negligence. Many times the interest and penalties will be as much as the taxes assessed. To keep your corporation from having these taxes assessed, you should work closely with your tax professional and attorney to make certain that you establish reasonable needs for the business that will justify any accumulation of earnings.

Personal Holding Company Tax

The Personal Holding Company tax is also 39.6% and is a tax in addition to the regular tax of the corporation. Therefore, if your corporate taxable income is between $100,000 and $335,000, your federal tax rate is 39%, the Personal Holding Company rate is 39.6%, and the state rate is probably at least 5%, the total tax that your corporation would be paying then is 83.6%.

This Personal Holding Company tax is figured on undistributed personal holding company income which generally is the taxable income of the corporation less the federal income taxes and dividends paid by the corporation. This tax is imposed on corporations which individuals have formed to receive, hold and reinvest income. Or they may use the corporation to receive compensation of the shareholders so that the income will be taxed at the corporate rate and not the shareholder's tax rate.

A Personal Holding Company is generally any corporation where (a) at least 60% of ordinary gross income as adjusted is personal holding company income, and (b) at any time during the latter half of the tax year, more than 50% in value of its outstanding stock is owned either directly or indirectly by not more than five individuals. The definition of an individual for this purpose is (a) a qualified pension profit-sharing, or stock bonus plan; (b) a trust that provides for the payment of supplemental unemployment compensation under certain conditions; (c) a private foundation; (d) or a part of a trust permanently set aside or used exclusively for the purpose described in section 642(c).

There are corporations excluded from the personal holding company tax even though the two requirements are met. A sub-chapter S corporation is not a personal holding company. Other corporations that are excluded are (a) tax-exempt corporations; (b) banks; (c) domestic building and loan associations; (d) life insurance companies; (e) surety companies; (f) foreign personal holding companies; (g) certain lending or finance companies. Also excluded are (h) some foreign corporations, if during the last half of the tax year all of the corporation's stock is owned by nonresident alien individuals; (i) certain small business investment companies; (j) corporations under court jurisdiction in a Title 11 or similar case; and (k) passive foreign investment companies.

The personal holding company income is the portion of adjusted ordinary gross income that generally consists of dividends, interest, royalties, annuities, rents, mineral royalties, oil royalties, gas royalties, copyright royalties, rents from the distribution and exhibition of produced films, compensation for the use of tangible property of the corporation, amounts received by a corporation from contracts for personal services, and income required to be reported by a corporate beneficiary from the income tax provisions relating to estates and trusts. Most of these items have exceptions used in calculating this income.

Also, in calculating the adjusted ordinary gross income,

there are four adjustments: (a) rental income is reduced by the deductions for depreciation and amortization, property taxes, interest, and rents paid that are applicable to this income; (b) income from mineral, oil, and gas royalties and from working interest in oil and gas wells is reduced for deductions for depreciation, amortization and depletion, property and severance taxes, interest, and rents paid that are applicable to this income; (c) interest on U. S. bonds held for sale by a dealer that is making a primary market for these bonds, and interest on condemnation awards, judgments, and tax refunds; and (d) rent received from the lease of tangible personal property manufactured by the taxpayer, who is engaged in substantial manufacturing or production of property of the same type, must be reduced by deductions for depreciation and amortization, taxes, rent and interest paid that are applicable to this income. Since this 60% test is based on adjusted ordinary gross income, all capital gains are excluded.

In determining stock ownership for this personal holding company tax, the constructive ownership rules apply, and they are very liberally interpreted by the IRS under five different categories. For instance, one of the constructive ownership rules states that an individual is considered as owner of the stock owned, directly or indirectly, by or for his family (whole or half-blooded brothers and sisters, spouse, ancestors, and lineal descendants), or by or for his partner. Based on this one rule, you can see that the interpretation by the IRS is very broad.

If the IRS determines that there is a deficiency in the personal holding company tax, the corporation can distribute deficiency dividends within 90 days after the deficiency determination has been made. Then they can file a claim for the deficiency dividend deduction within 120 days of the determination of the deficiency by the IRS.

The personal holding company tax is calculated on Schedule PH. This is a two page form and is attached to Form 1120. There are eight pages of instructions for the determination of whether this tax is due, and for the preparation of this form. Since there are many complicated calculations that you must make to see if your corporation is subject to this tax, and there are many adjustments that you must make to your corporation's taxable income, you should be sure to obtain the detailed instructions for calculating and preparing this form. As with the other taxes that I have discussed in this chapter, it would be wise for you to discuss your corporate transactions with your professional tax advisor so that you can determine if your corporation is subject to this very high personal holding company tax.

As with the other taxes, the IRS may assess your corporation for a three-year period for this tax. You will also have interest to pay, as well as the related penalties that may accrue. As stated before, the interest and penalties may be as much or more than the tax, so with the tax being 83.6%, you may end up paying more taxes, interest, and penalty than you have in net income for these three years.

Since an S corporation is not a personal holding company, you might consider making the S corporation election if it appears that you are going to have a problem with this tax. Also, an S corporation election may help to eliminate your accumulated earnings tax. Most taxpayers do not realize that they have problems with the personal holding company tax and the accumulated earnings tax until the IRS audits their corporate tax returns. At that time, it is too late to make the S corporation election for the back years.

So that you will not be stacked with taxes by the IRS, you must do proper tax planning on a continuing basis, and because of the complexity of the taxes discussed in this chapter, your professional tax advisor should be consulted on a regular basis.

Chapter 12

Give Me What's Mine!

WHEN WE PREPARE OUR ANNUAL TAX RETURNS, we may know about all of the itemized deductions that we can use on our returns. We may also know about all of the deductions that can be used on our business, farm and rental schedules; however, we may not be aware of all of the credits that individuals, businesses, and corporations may be able to use to deduct against any income taxes that may be owed.

These credits are either nonrefundable or refundable credits. The nonrefundable credits can reduce your federal income tax to zero, but any amount of credit over your income tax will not be refunded to you. The refundable credits are treated as payments, and they are added to the amount of federal income tax that you have had withheld. If the credit is more than your taxes due, the excess is refunded to you.

Individual Tax Credits

For individuals, there are six types of nonrefundable tax credits that I will discuss in this chapter. These are (a) child and dependent care credit; (b) credit for the elderly or the disabled; (c) credit for prior year minimum tax; (d) mortgage interest credit; (e) credit for electric vehicles; and (f) foreign tax credit.

Also, for individuals, there are four types of refundable tax credits that I will cover. They are (a) earned income credit; (b) credit for excess social security tax or railroad retirement tax withheld; (c) credit from a regulated investment company; and (d) credit on diesel-powered highway vehicles.

Individual Nonrefundable Tax Credits

The child and dependent care credit can be claimed on Form 2441 for the child and dependent care you pay each year so that you can work or look for work. This care must be for one or more qualifying persons who live in your home with you, and these qualifying persons are usually children or parents. You must have earned income and are able to use $2,400 of the payments to calculate the tax credit for one qualifying person, and $4,800 of the payments to calculate the tax credit for two or more qualifying persons. The percentage of the tax credit varies with adjusted gross income, but it does not drop below 20% in calculating the credit. If you have two children and pay $4,800 for their care during the year, the minimum amount of credit that you will be able to claim is (20% x $4,800) $960. On Form 2441, you must provide the name, address, and social security number of the care provider, and this care provider cannot be anyone that you claim as a dependent on your return. If the care provider keeps your children in your home, you may be required to withhold employment taxes and file quarterly household employees tax returns. Most taxpayers want this credit, but they do not want anything to do with filing and paying these quarterly taxes. There are special rules for qualifying persons and for keeping up a home that are explained in detail in IRS Publication 503 and in the instructions for completing Form 2441.

The credit for the elderly or the disabled can amount to $750 for an individual or $1,125 for a married couple. It can be claimed if you are age 65 or older or are retired on permanent and total disability and are under the age of 65. Permanent and total disability means that you are unable to engage in any substantial gainful employment activity because of your physical or mental condition. A physician must certify that your permanent and total disability condition has lasted or can be expected to last continuously for twelve months or more or that this condition can be expected to result in death. The base amount for calculating the credit is reduced by your nontaxable social security or railroad retirement benefits, and other nontaxable pensions and disability benefits that you receive. This base amount also is reduced as your adjusted gross income increases. If you are able to benefit from this credit, you can obtain additional information from IRS Publication 524 Credit for the Elderly or the Disabled and from the instructions for Schedule R that is used to calculate this credit.

You may be able to take a credit for prior year minimum tax if you paid alternative minimum tax during the prior year, have an unused minimum tax credit that you are carrying forward from the prior year, or have certain unallowed credits from the prior year. This credit is calculated on Form 8801, and there are detail instructions for preparing this form.

You can claim a mortgage interest credit if you were issued a mortgage credit certificate (MCC) under a qualified MCC program by your state or local government. The certificate must be used in connection with the purchase, qualified rehabilitation, or qualified home improvement of your main home. The credit rate and the maximum loan amounts are shown on the MCC. If the certificate credit rate is more than 20%, the credit cannot be more than $2,000. If you itemize your deductions on Schedule A, you must reduce your home mortgage interest deduction by the amount of the credit. This credit is calculated on Form 8396, and there are detail instructions for preparing this form.

You may be eligible for a 10% tax credit if you placed a qualified electric vehicle in service during the year. The credit is 10% of the cost of the vehicle and is limited to $4,000 for each vehicle. A qualified electric vehicle is a vehicle that has at least four wheels and can be driven on public streets and highways. It is powered primarily by an electric motor, was originally purchased and used by you, and is not for resale. This credit can be claimed on Form 8834, and there are also detailed instructions for this form.

The last nonrefundable tax credit that I will discuss is the foreign tax credit. If you paid or accrued taxes during the year to a foreign country or a United States possession, you can elect to use this tax as a credit against your income taxes or deduct them as an itemized deduction. The income has to be included in your taxable income during the year. Many taxpayers have this foreign tax on mutual fund statements that they receive from their investment company and are not using the credit against their income taxes. This tax credit is claimed on Form 1116. There are instructions for this form, and Publication 514 has more detailed instructions for completing this form and claiming the credit.

Individual Refundable Tax Credits

The first refundable tax credit that I will discuss is the earned income tax credit. This credit is referred to by the tax professional as a negative income tax, since the taxpayer can obtain a relatively large refund and may have no federal income tax withheld from his pay. This tax credit is probably more widely used and more widely abused than any other tax credit or any other item on the individual tax returns. However, this tax credit is often overlooked by taxpayers who have had a temporary decrease in income, as they have generally been higher than average income earners in past years. This credit can be claimed by taxpayers that have adjusted gross income that does not exceed the upper mid-twenty thousand dollars and has a qualifying child who lived with them. You must have earned income during the year; therefore, if your income is only composed of interest, dividends and rental income, you would not qualify. Your qualifying child must be your child, a descendant of your child, a stepchild, an adopted child, or an eligible foster child. An adopted child is one that has been placed with you for adoption by an authorized placement agency. An eligible foster child may include a brother, sister, nephew, niece, cousin, or others who have lived with you and was a member of your household for the whole year. You must have provided care for this foster child as you would your own child. A child, other than a foster child, must have lived with you for more than half the year to meet the residency test. There is an age test that the qualifying child must meet. The child must be under age 19 at the end of the year or must be a full-time student under age 24 at the end of the year, or must be permanently and totally disabled at any time during the year, regardless of age. If your qualifying child is age 1 or over at the end of the year, you must provide a correct and valid social security number for each child listed on your return. If a child does not have a social security number, you should apply for one on Form SS-5 from the Social Security Administration. It usually takes approximately two weeks to receive this social security number. If you do not provide a correct and valid social security number, your refund will be delayed for several weeks or months. Beginning in 1994, a taxpayer without a qualifying child who is at least age 25 but under age 65 before the end of the tax year, and had income under $9,000 could receive a tax credit of up to $306. To claim this credit, either with or without a qualifying child, you should complete Schedule EIC. Detailed instructions for filing this schedule are found in Publication 596, and also accompany the schedule.

Another refundable tax credit is the credit for excess social security tax or railroad retirement tax withheld. If you or your spouse worked for two or more employers during the year, and these employers paid you wages over the amounts that are subject to social security and railroad retirement taxes, you will be able to claim the excess amount of tax withheld on those wages as a tax credit against your federal income tax. Any excess tax credit above the amount of your tax liability will be refunded to you. If you have only one employer, and this employer withholds social security or railroad retirement taxes in excess of the wage limit amount, you will not be able to claim this excess amount withheld by your employer as a credit against your income taxes. This excess amount must be paid back to you by your employer. The refundable tax credit for this excess social security tax or railroad retirement tax is claimed in the payments section of Form 1040, page 2, and it is included in the total amount of the federal income taxes withheld and paid.

The tax credit from a regulated investment company is shown on Form 2439 that the investment company or mutual fund mails to you. This form shows the undistributed capital gains and any taxes that have been paid thereon. You will include the income on your tax return for any capital gain distributions allocated to you even though you may not have received the distribution amount. This refundable tax credit is also shown in the payments section of Form 1040, page 2, and it is included in the total amount of the federal income taxes withheld and paid.

There is a refundable tax credit for diesel-powered highway vehicles. This is a one-time credit that can be claimed by you if you are the first owner of the diesel vehicle, and you did not purchase the vehicle for resale. The credit amounts to $102 for a diesel-powered automobile, or $198 for diesel-powered light van or truck. Most taxpayers are not claiming this credit because many times the taxpayer does not tell the tax professional that the vehicle that has been purchased during the year is diesel-powered. The credit is claimed on Form 4136, and additional instructions for filing this form is found in Publication 378.

General Business Tax Credits

The general business tax credits are generated though your trade or business. Your trade or business may be a sole-ownership, a partnership, or a corporation. The seven general business tax credits that I will discuss in this chapter are (a) investment credit; (b) targeted jobs credit; (c) alcohol fuels credit; (d) research and experimental credit; (e) low-income housing credit; (f) disabled access credit; and (g) enhanced oil recovery credit. These general business tax credits are generally limited to your net income tax liability for the year, and for higher income taxpayers other limitations apply. For any unused tax credit, you can generally carry the unused portion back three years and forward for fifteen years. Use Form 1040X or Form 1045 to carry this credit back for individuals, and Form 1120X or Form 1139 to carry this credit back for corporations. The carryover of this credit is claimed on Form 3800.

Most taxpayers think that the investment tax credit is no longer available, and the investment tax credit on business machinery and equipment has expired. However, investment tax credit for reforestation, certain building rehabilitation, and energy credit is still available. You can take a 10% reforestation credit on up to $10,000 of expenses each year to plant a forest or reforest property you have for growing trees for sale or commercial production of timber products. The expenses must qualify for amortization; however, you can take the investment credit for this reforestation expense whether you choose to amortize the expense or add the expense to the basis of your property. You can take a rehabilitation credit for the renovation, restoration, or reconstruction for buildings placed in service before 1936, and for certified historic structures. This credit does not apply to expenses for the enlargement or new construction for these buildings. There is a 10% credit for buildings placed in service before 1936, and a 20% credit for certified historic structures. The energy credit applies to certain expenditures for solar or geothermal energy property that you have placed in service during the year. This energy credit is 10% of the related expenses. The reforestation credit, the rehabilitation credit, and the energy credit are placed on Form 3468. You reduce the depreciable basis of the assets on which these credits are taken. The reduced basis is 100% of the rehabilitation credit and 50% of the reforestation and energy credits. There are detailed instructions for completing Form 3468 and Form 3800.

The targeted jobs tax credit is being replaced with the Work Opportunity Tax Credit (WOTC) in the Balanced Budget Reconciliation Act of 1995. This WOTC credit will amount to 35% of a qualified workers first $6,000 of wages. The qualified employees, other than summer youth, must work at least 400 hours or 180 days before the credit can be claimed. Summer youths must work 120 hours or 20 days before the credit can be claimed. You must hire from five targeted groups to be able to claim this credit. The five targeted groups are individuals on AFDC, qualified veterans on food stamps, ex-felons, high-risk youth, a vocational rehabilitation referral, and a qualified summer youth employee.

There is an alcohol fuel tax credit for sellers of straight alcohol and alcohol mixtures that will be used as fuel. The credit is up to $.60 per gallon for straight alcohol and alcohol mixture, and $.10 per gallon for small ethanol producers. The credit can be taken only by the seller or producer, and it is not taken by the buyer even though the fuel may be used in the buyer's business. This alcohol credit is calculated on Form 6478, and then is carried to Form 3800 and becomes part of the general business credit. There are detailed instructions for completing Form 6478.

The research and experimental credit is used to encourage businesses to increase their expenditures on research and experimental activities. The research tax credit is 20% of the amount by which your research expenses for the year exceed a base amount. This base amount can not be less than half of the expenditures for the current year. Generally, if your company begins research and experimental work this year and spends $100,000, you would calculate your credit, with a few modifications as $100,000 x 50% = $50,000 x 20% = $10,000. To generally be able to claim this credit year after year, your expenditures for research and experimental items must continue to be more than the expenditures for the prior year or years. This credit is claimed on Form 6765, and there are detailed instructions for filing this form.

The low-income housing credit is designed to provide affordable housing for low-income individuals. This credit applies to qualified low-income housing that was placed in service after 1986, and it is one of just a few tax shelters that has not been completely eliminated for the higher income taxpayer. The credit is calculated on Form 8586, and there are some very detailed instructions for this form and for calculating the credit.

The disabled access credit is for expenses paid by small businesses to comply with the Americans with Disabilities Act of 1990. These expenses are to provide access to persons with disabilities by removing architectural, communication, physical, and transportation barriers. The expenses are also for providing other similar services, modifications, materials, and equipment for persons with disabilities, including persons with hearing and visual impairments. The eligible small businesses are those with 30 or fewer full-time employees, or with $1 million or less in gross receipts. The credit is 50% of the eligible expenses that do not exceed $10,250, with the first $250 of expenses excluded. This will give you a maximum credit of $5,000. This credit is claimed on Form 8826, and there are detailed instructions for completing this form. I encourage all eligible small businesses to take advantage of this large credit before congress decides to eliminate it. If you, some family member, or a friend has some form of disability, you realize the importance of these expenditures for your business.

The enhanced oil recovery credit is 15% of the qualified costs for enhanced oil recovery projects in the United States. There are nine recovery methods listed in the June 1979 Department of Energy regulations that are considered as qualified enhanced oil recovery projects. The credit is claimed on Form 8830, and there are detailed instructions for this form.

Other credits that are generally available for your trade or business, but have not been written about in this chapter, are renewable electricity production credit, empowerment zone employment credit, Indian employment credit, credit for employer social security and medicare taxes paid on certain employee tips, and credit for contributions to selected community development corporations. There are forms for calculating each of these credits and detailed instructions for completing these forms.

The credits that I have discussed in this chapter will help

to reduce your tax liability considerably each year. With proper planning, the credits can be used over a number of years, so that you will receive more credit in years with higher taxes. Many of the tax credits and instructions are very complex, and you may need to work with your tax professional to help develop your tax strategy for using these credits.

EXAMPLES

EXAMPLE CORRESPONDENCE LETTER TO IRS

EXAMPLE 1

(DATE)

Internal Revenue Service Center
Memphis, TN. 37501

Re: Taxpayer(s) Name(s)
Social Security Number:
Tax Period:

Dear Internal Revenue Service:

I(we) have enclosed a copy of the following items:
(A) Your notice to me (us) dated ________ showing that I (we) owe you additional tax, penalty and interest of $1,250.
(B) Copy of my (our) page 1 & 2 of Form 1040, Schedule A, B, and my business Schedule C.
(C) My (our) check for $177.50 that represents the correct amount of tax that I (we) owe to the IRS based on the amount we have recalculated directly on your enclosed notice.

You state in your notice to me (us) that the amount of interest expense that has been claimed on the Schedule A itemized deduction exceeded the amount reported to you by the various financial institution on Forms 1098 by $750. Please see enclosed Form 1098 from our bank showing in fact that I (we) have this $750 correctly reported on Schedule A.

You also show that I (we) have not shown $1,000 of interest income from our bank that was reported to you on their Form 1099INT. I (we) contacted the bank and received the enclosed copy of the Form 1099INT in question and found that the bank had the incorrect address shown thereon, so this form was never received by us and therefore, not reported on my (our) return. The correct tax and interest of $177.50 has been enclosed for payment of this item.

You show that I (we) have not properly picked up the $3,000 of income from Form 1099 sent to you from ABC Mfg. Co., Inc. on my (our) Schedule C attached. The gross income reported on Schedule C is for $33,000, with $30,000 being reported to IRS from XYZ Mfg. Co., Inc., and the balance of $3,000 is the amount shown on the enclosed Form 1099 from ABC Mfg. Co., Inc.

After you adjust your records to show that I (we) only owe the enclosed $177.50, please notify me (us) by return mail that no additional tax, penalty or interest is due on my (our) return.

Very truly yours,

Taxpayer(s) Name(s)

Enclosures

EXAMPLE OF SECOND LETTER TO IRS

EXAMPLE 2

(DATE)

Internal Revenue Service Center
Memphis, TN. 37501

Re: Taxpayer(s) Name(s)
Social Security Number:
Tax Year:

Dear Internal Revenue Service:

I (we) have enclosed a copy of the following items:
(A) Your notice to me (us) dated__________showing that I (we) still owe $1,250 and that I (we) have not previously corresponded with you.
(B) My (our) letter to you dated ________ along with all attached data showing that only $177.50 was owed to the IRS.

As stated in my (our) previous letter to you, the only tax, penalty and interest owed was $177.50, and a check for that amount was forwarded to you with my (our) previous letter.

As previously requested, please correct your records to show that I (we) owe no additional tax, penalty and interest and please notify me (us) by return mail that you have made the corrections requested.

Very truly yours,

Taxpayer(s) Name(s)

Enclosures

CC: Problems Resolution
Internal Revenue Service
P. O. Box 30309
Memphis, TN. 38130

EXAMPLE CORRESPONDENCE TO IRS PROBLEMS RESOLUTION

EXAMPLE 3

(DATE)

Problems Resolution
Internal Revenue Service
P. O. Box 30309
Memphis, TN. 38130

Re: Taxpayer(s) Name(s)
Social Security Number:
Tax Year:

Dear Problems Resolution:

I (we) have enclosed all of the previous correspondence with the IRS Service Center and ask that you review the documents that we have provided two times to the IRS Service Center, and I (we) would appreciate your help in resolving the items in question.

Please let me (us) know if we need to provide you with any additional information.

Very truly yours,

Taxpayer(s) Name(s)

Enclosures

EXAMPLE OF IRS T-ACCOUNT
EXAMPLE 4

Source or Receipt of Money		Application or payment of money	
Cash on Hand- 01/01	$500	Cash on Hand-12/31	$1,000
Cash in Bank-01/01	$10,000	Cash in Bank-12/31	$20,000
CDs-01/01	$20,000	CDs-12/31	$30,000
W-2 Wages-Net	$40,000		
Dividends	$1,000		
Interest	$1,000		
Schedule C Net Income Less Depreciation	$10,000		
Schedule D Receipts	$5,000		
Schedule E Receipts	$0		
Schedule F Receipts	$0		
Loans Made During Year	$0	Loans Paid During Year	$22,500
Gifts	$0		
Assets Sold	$0		
Inheritances	$0		
Other Income	$0	Personal Living Expenses	$24,000
Total Sources and Money Received	$87,500	Total Application and Payment of Money	$97,500
		Less: Sources and Money Received	$87,500
		Understatement of Income	$10,000

EXAMPLE 5

Information About Your Notice, Penalty and Interest

Department of the Treasury
Internal Revenue Service
Notice 746 (Rev. 7-95)
Catalog Number 63146F

The interest rates on underpayment and overpayment of taxes are as follows:

Periods	**Percentage Rates**	
	Underpayment	Overpayment
January 1, 1987, through September 30, 1987	9	8
October 1, 1987, through December 31, 1987	10	9
January 1, 1988, through March 31, 1988	11	10
April 1, 1988, through September 30, 1988	10	9
October 1, 1988, through March 31, 1989	11	10
April 1, 1989, through September 30, 1989	12	11
October 1, 1989, through March 31, 1991	11	10
April 1, 1991, through December 31, 1991	10	9
January 1, 1992, through March 31, 1992	9	8
April 1, 1992 through September 30, 1992	8	7
October 1, 1992 through June 30, 1994	7	6
July 1, 1994 through September 30, 1994	8	7
October 1, 1994 through March 31, 1995	9	8
April 1, 1995 through June 30, 1995	10	9
Beginning July 1, 1995	9	8

Beginning January 1, 1987, the interest rate we pay on your overpayment of taxes is one percent less than the rate of interest we charge on your underpayment of taxes. The law requires us to redetermine these interest rates quarterly.

We compound interest daily except on estimated taxes for individuals or corporations.

We charge a special interest rate of 120 percent of the underpayment rate if:

— The return, not including extensions, is due before January 1, 1990,
— The underpayment is more than $1,000, and
— The underpayment came from a tax-motivated transaction.

We charge interest on penalties for late filing, over or understating valuations, and substantially understating the tax you owe. Also, we charge interest on fraud and negligence penalties if the tax returns, including extensions, are due after December 31, 1988.

We will continue to charge interest until you pay the amount you owe in full.
After December 31, 1990, the law allows us to charge interest at the underpayment rate plus two percent on underpayments of more than $100,000 for large (C) corporations.

If you receive a bill, refund, or other notice from the Internal Revenue Service, you may call us at your local IRS office for an explanation. The code numbers on the notice you received match the code numbers of the paragraphs below. All days mentioned in these explanations are calendar days, unless **specifically** stated otherwise.

Removal of Penalties

Reasonable Cause. The law lets us remove or reduce the penalties we explain in this notice if you have an acceptable reason. If you believe you have an acceptable reason, you may send us a signed statement explaining your reason. We will review it and let you know if we accept your explanation as reasonable cause to remove or reduce your penalty. This procedure doesn't apply to interest and, in some cases, we may ask you to pay the tax in full before we reduce or remove the penalty for paying late.

Erroneous Written Advice from IRS.

We will also remove your penalty if:

— you wrote to IRS and asked for advice on a specific issue,

— you gave IRS complete and accurate information,

— IRS wrote back to you and gave you a specific course of action to take or explained what actions not to take,

— you followed our written advice in the manner we outlined, and

— you were penalized for the written advice we gave you.

To have the penalty removed because of erroneous written advice from IRS, you should:

— complete Form 843, Claim for Refund and Request for Abatement,

— request that IRS remove the penalty, and

— send Form 843 to the IRS Service Center where you filed your return for the year you relied on erroneous advice from the IRS.

The three documents you must attach to your Form 843 are:

— a copy of your original request for advice from IRS,

— a copy of the erroneous written advice from IRS, and

— a notice (if any) showing the penalty we charged that you now wish us to remove.

01 **Filing and Paying Late**—We charged a 5% combined penalty of 4 1/2% for filing late and 1/2% for paying late because, according to our records, you filed your return late and didn't pay your tax by the due date of your return. The combined penalty is 5% of your unpaid tax for each month or part of a month your return is late, but not for more than 5 months, which would total 25% (22 1/2% late filing and 2 1/2 late paying).

In addition to the 22 1/2% late filing penalty for the first 5 months your return is late, we continue to charge the 1/2% late paying penalty for each month or part of a month for as long as your tax is unpaid, but not for more than 25%. Therefore, the maximum penalty we can charge is 47 1/2% (22 1/2% late filing plus 25% late paying).

If you didn't file your return within 60 days of the due date, the minimum penalty is $100 or 100% of the balance of tax due on your tax return, whichever is smaller. If you think we should remove or reduce this penalty, *see "Removal of Penalty — Reasonable Cause."*

02 **Underpayment or Late Payment of Estimated Tax** — We charged you a penalty because, according to our records, you didn't estimate your tax and pay the correct amount of tax due.

Individuals, Estates, and Certain Trusts — If you expect to owe tax of $500 or more for the tax year, you must prepay the tax by having tax withheld or by making estimated tax payments. We charge a penalty when the total tax you pay in during the year doesn't meet the requirements of the law. The requirements for the last several tax years are as follows.

For 1994 and later, if your adjusted gross income in the preceding taxable year is more than $150,000 (more than $75,000 if your filing status is married filing separately), your total estimated tax payments must equal 110% of the tax shown on your return for the preceding year or 90% of the tax shown on the return for the current year, whichever is less.

For 1992 and 1993, you are required to pay at least 90% of the tax shown on your return for the current year or 100% of the tax shown on your return for the prior year, whichever is less. However, the law requires certain taxpayers (other than farmers and fishermen) to use a special computation when basing their current year estimated tax payments on 100% of their prior year tax. You must use this special computation if all the following apply to you:

1) You made an estimated tax payment for any of your three prior tax years, or we charged you a penalty for not paying estimated tax for any of your three prior tax years. (Don't include withholding or a credit from your prior year's tax as a payment of estimated tax.)

2) Your adjusted gross income (AGI) as shown on your return for the current year is more than $75,000 (more than $37,500 if your filing status is married filing separately).

3) Your modified AGI for the current tax year (as defined in the instructions for Form 2210, Underpayment of Estimated Tax for Individuals and Fiduciaries) will exceed the AGI shown on your prior year tax return by more than $40,000 (more than $20,000 if you are married filing separately).

If all the above conditions apply to you, you may base only your first estimated tax payment on 100% of your prior year's tax. However, you must base your second installment on 90% of the tax shown on your current year return plus the difference between that amount and the amount of your first payment. You must base your remaining payments on 90% of the tax shown on your return for the current year so that the total estimated tax paid for the year will equal at least 90%.

You will not be charged a penalty if you make your payments in sufficient amounts and on time. In addition, because we lowered the withholding rates in 1992, you won't be charged a penalty if:

1) the only reason you underestimated and underpaid your tax was because we lowered the withholding rates, and

2) the amount you owe is $146 or less if you filed as single or head of household ($292 or less if you filed as married filing joint return or married filing separately).

For 1985 through 1991, you were required to pay at least 90% of the tax shown on your current year's return or 100% of the tax shown on your prior year's return, whichever was less.

For 1985 through 1987, you were required to meet one of the four exceptions to the penalty listed on Form 2210, Underpayment of Estimated Tax by Individuals and Fiduciaries.

For 1984, you were required to meet one of the conditions explained in the instructions for Form 2210, under the heading "Waiver of Penalty."

For more information on when the estimated tax penalty may be reduced or removed, see the instructions for Form 2210 for your tax year.

Corporations— We charge a penalty for not estimating your tax correctly when the corporation owes $500 or more in tax, and the total payments made on time are less than the required amount.

For tax years beginning after December 31, 1993, the law requires corporations to pay the lesser of 100% of the prior year tax or 100% of the tax estimated for the current year through quarterly tax payments.

For tax years beginning after June 30, 1992, and before January 1, 1994, the law requires corporations to pay the lesser of 100% of the prior year tax or 97% of the tax estimated for the current year through quarterly estimated tax payments.

For tax years beginning after December 31, 1991, and before July 1, 1992, the law requires corporations to pay the lesser of 100% of the prior year tax or 93% of the tax estimated for the current year through quarterly payments.

For tax years beginning after December 31, 1987, and before January 1, 1992, the law requires corporations to pay the lesser of 90% of the tax shown on the current tax return or 100% of the tax shown for the prior year.

For tax years beginning before January 1, 1988, the 100% of the prior year tax rule doesn't apply as an exception to the penalty. However, we may remove or whichever is greater. For checks of less than $15, the penalty is the check amount. If you think we should remove or reduce this penalty, see *"Removal of Penalty — Reasonable Cause."*

05 **Fraud** — We charged you a penalty for fraud. The penalty is 75% of the tax you didn't pay due to fraud (50% of the tax you didn't pay due to fraud on returns required to be filed before January 1, 1987,not including extensions).

For tax you didn't pay due to fraud on returns required to be filed before January 1, 1989, the penalty includes an additional 50% of the interest charged on the part of your underpayment due to fraud. This additional interest charge is a penalty and you cannot deduct it from your federal taxes.

06 **Negligence Penalty** — We charged a penalty of 5% on your unpaid tax. For underpayments on returns due before January 1, 1989, not including extensions, we charged an additional 50% of the interest on the part of your underpayment due to negligence. This additional interest charge is a penalty and you cannot deduct it from your federal taxes.

07 **Paying Late** — We charged a penalty because, according to our records, you didn't pay your tax on time. Initially, the penalty is 1/2% of the unpaid tax for each month or part of a month you didn't pay your tax.

If we issue a Notice of Intent to Levy and you don't pay the balance due within 10 days from the date of the notice, the penalty increases to 1% a month.

The penalty can't be more than 25% of the tax paid late. If you think we should remove or reduce this penalty, see *"Removal of Penalty — Reasonable Cause."*

08 **Missing Taxpayer Identifying Number (TIN)** — We charge a penalty when you don't provide a social security number (SSN) for yourself, your dependent, or another person. We also charge a penalty when you don't provide your own SSN to day after the date of the first notice we sent you asking for the tax you owe.

We figured your penalty using one of the rates listed above. **When you don't pay the amount you owe within ten days of the date of the first notice we sent you, we automatically increase the penalty rate to 15%** and include the additional penalty in your next bill.

If you believe we computed the penalty incorrectly, please send a complete breakdown of your tax liability by filling in the enclosed Form 4977 (for tax years before 1993), or Form 941, Schedule B (for tax years 1993 and later). If you think we should remove or reduce this penalty, see *"Removal of Penalty — Reasonable Cause."* Also see Publication 15, *Circular E — Employer's Tax Guide,* for deposit requirements.

12 **Incomplete Return** — We charged a penalty because, according to our records, you didn't file a complete return. The penalty is $10 a day for each day the return was incomplete, but may not be more than $5,000 or 5% of your gross receipts for the year, whichever is less. If you think we should remove or reduce this penalty, see *"Removal of Penalty — Reasonable Cause."*

14 **Fraud — Late Filing Penalty** — The law allows us to increase the penalty for filing late if you didn't file on time because of fraud. The penalty is 15% of the amount of tax you should have reported on your tax return and an additional 15% for each additional month or part of a month you didn't file your return. The total penalty may not be more than 75% of the tax you didn't pay.

17 **Penalty Removed** — We removed the penalty we charged you, and we are reviewing your account. We will let you know the results.

27 **Penalty on Tips** — We charged a penalty because, according to our records, you didn't report your tips to your employer. The

reduce this penalty if you meet any of the exceptions on Form 2220, Underpayment of Estimated Tax by Corporations.

The procedures for reasonable cause do not apply to corporate estimated tax penalties. For more information on when the estimated tax penalty may be reduced or removed, see Form 2220 and its instructions for your tax year. The procedures for reasonable cause don't apply to corporate estimated tax penalties.

03 **Failure to Deposit — Federal Tax Deposits Insufficient/Late** — We charged a penalty because it appears that you didn't deposit the correct amounts of tax on time. We used your Record of Tax Liability to determine where to apply your deposits. We applied your deposits in the date order we received them. We figured the penalty on any tax not deposited, deposited late, or not deposited in the correct amounts.

For deposits due after December 31, 1989, the penalty rate varies as follows:

2% — deposits made 1 to 5 days late,
5% — deposits made 6 to 15 days late,
10% — deposits made 16 days or more late, but on or before the 10th day after the date of the first notice we sent you asking for the tax you owe.

We figured your penalty using one of the rates listed above. **When you don't pay the amount you owe within ten days of the date of the first notice we sent you, we automatically increase the penalty rate to 15%** and include the additional penalty in your next bill.

If you think we should remove or reduce this penalty, see *"Removal of Penalty — Reasonable Cause."* Also see Publication 15, *Circular E — Employer's Tax Guide*, for deposit requirements.

04 **Dishonored Check** — We charged a penalty because your bank didn't honor your check. For checks of $15 or more, the penalty is $15 or 2% of your check amount, another person, or if you don't include your employer identification number on an information return.

The penalty is $5 for each missing TIN the law requires on returns and statements due by December 31, 1989. The penalty is $50 for each missing TIN the law requires on returns and statements due after December 31, 1989.

For all missing TINs in any calendar year, the penalty can't be more than $100,000. If you think we should remove or reduce this penalty, see *"Removal of Penalty — Reasonable Cause."*

10 **Filing Late — Exempt Organizations and Certain Trusts** — We charged a penalty because, according to our records, you filed your return late. The penalty is $10 a day for each day your return is late, but may not be more than $5,000 or 5% of your gross receipts for the year, whichever is less. If you think we should remove or reduce this penalty, see *"Removal of Penalty — Reasonable Cause."*

11 **Failure to Deposit — Federal Tax Deposits Insufficient/Late and Incomplete Record of Federal Tax Liability** — We charged a penalty because it appears that you didn't deposit the correct amounts of tax on time.

Also, your Record of Federal Tax Liability was incomplete or illegible, or the liability amounts you reported didn't equal the net taxes for the tax period. Therefore, we averaged the total tax liability and distributed it equally throughout the tax period. We applied your deposits to the averaged liabilities in the date order we received them. We figured the penalty on any tax not deposited, deposited late, or not deposited in the correct amounts.

For deposits due after December 31, 1989, the penalty rate is as follows:

2% — deposits made 1 to 5 days late,
5% — deposits made 6 to 15 days late,
10% — deposits made 16 or more days late, but on or before the 10th

penalty is 50% of the social security or railroad retirement tax on the tips you didn't report. If you think we should remove or reduce this penalty, see *"Removal of Penalty — Reasonable Cause."*

28 **Examining Officer's Report** — According to our records, your Examining Officer gave you a report that explained the reason for this penalty.

30 **Late Payment Penalty Removed** — We removed the late payment penalty we previously charged you.

31 **False W-4 Penalty** — We charged a $500 penalty because it appears you made false statements on your Form W-4. If you think we are wrong, or that we should remove or reduce this penalty for any reason, see *"Removal of Penalty — Reasonable Cause."*

32 **Partnership Late Filing** — We charged the maximum penalty because, according to our records, you filed your partnership return late. The penalty is $50 for each person who was a partner at any time during the tax year, for each month or part of a month the return was filed late, for up to 5 months. If you think we should remove or reduce this penalty, see *"Removal of Penalty — Reasonable Cause."*

33-39 and 45-52 Filing Incomplete Return — We charged the maximum penalty because, according to our records, your partnership return was incomplete, and you didn't give us the information we requested. The penalty is $50 for each person who was a partner at any time during the tax year, for each month or part of a month for up to 5 months.

If you think we should remove or reduce this penalty, see *"Removal of Penalty — Reasonable Cause."*

33 — Missing Schedules K-1.
34 — Missing Schedule L (Balance Sheets)
35 — Missing Schedule K-1 TINs (5 or more)

36 — Missing Schedules K-1 and Schedule L (Balance Sheets)
37 — Missing Schedules K-1 and Schedule K-1 TINs
38 — Missing Schedule L (Balance Sheet) and Schedule K-1 TINs
39 — Missing Schedules K-1, Schedule K-1 TINs, and Schedule L (Balance Sheets)
45 — Missing Schedules K
46 — Missing Schedules K and Schedules K-1
47 — Missing Schedules K and Schedules L (Balance Sheets)
48 — Missing Schedules K and Schedule K-1 TINs (5 or more)
49 — Missing Schedules K, Schedules K-1, and Schedules L (Balance Sheets)
50 — Missing Schedules K, Schedules K-1, and Schedule K-1 TINs
51 — Missing Schedules K, Schedules L (Balance Sheets), and Schedule K-1 TINs
52 — Missing Schedules K, Schedules K-1, Schedules L (Balance Sheets), and Schedule K-1 TINs (5 or more)

40 **Overstatement, Understatement, or Accuracy-Related Penalty** — For returns due before January 1, 1990, this penalty is one or more of the following: Valuation Overstatement, Valuation Understatement, or Substantial Understatement. For returns due after December 31, 1989, the accuracy-related penalty has been added. Refer to our Examining Officer's report for an explanation of the penalty.

41 **Failure to Deposit — Taxes Paid Directly to IRS** — We charged a penalty because, according to our records, you paid your taxes to an unauthorized financial institution, directly to the IRS, or with your return. The penalty is 10% of each payment you didn't deposit properly.

There is a limit to the amount of tax you may pay with your return. See the list below.

we averaged the total tax liability and distributed it equally throughout the tax period.

We applied your deposits and payments to the averaged liabilities in the date order we received your deposits. We figured the penalty on any tax deposited in the correct amounts.

If you believe we computed the penalty incorrectly, please send us a complete breakdown of your tax liability by filling in the enclosed Form 4977 (for tax years before 1993), or Form 941, Schedule B (for tax years 1993 and later). For additional details see **Information on Failure to Deposit Penalty,** Code 56.

44 **Failure To Deposit — Insufficient Late Deposits and Taxes Paid Directly to IRS and Record of Federal Tax Liability Incomplete** — We charged a penalty because, according to our records:

— you didn't make your tax deposit on time or in the correct amounts,
— you made one or more of your deposits to an unauthorized financial institution, paid your tax directly to the IRS or paid the tax with your return, and
— your Record of Federal Tax Liability was incomplete or illegible, or the liability amounts you reported didn't equal the net taxes for the tax period.

We averaged your total tax liability and distributed it equally throughout the tax period. Then we applied your deposits and payments to the averaged liabilities in the date order we received your deposits. We figured the penalty on any tax not deposited, deposited late, or not deposited in the correct amounts.

If you believe we computed the penalty incorrectly, please send us a complete breakdown of your tax liability by filling in the enclosed Form 4977 (for tax years before 1993), or Form 941, Schedule B (for tax years 1993 and later). For additional details see **Information on Failure to Deposit Penalty,** Code 56.

If you believe we computed the penalty incorrectly, please complete the enclosed Form 941, Schedule B. If you think we should remove or reduce this penalty, see "*Removal of Penalty — Reasonable Cause.*" For information on deposit requirements, see Publication 15, *Circular E — Employer's Tax Guide*, or Publication 51, *Circular A — Agricultural Employer's Tax Guide*.

55 **Failure to Deposit — Incorrect Record of Federal Tax Liability and Taxes Paid Directly to IRS** — We charged a penalty because your Form 941, Schedule B was incomplete and we couldn't determine if you made your deposits on time or in the correct amounts.

Therefore, we averaged the liability you reported, distributed it equally, and applied your deposits in the date order we received them. We figured the penalty on any tax not deposited, deposited late, or not deposited in the correct amounts.

Also, it appears that you paid taxes to an unauthorized financial institution, directly to the IRS, or with your tax return.

If you believe we computed the penalty incorrectly, please complete the enclosed Form 941, Schedule B. For additional details see **Information on Failure to Deposit Penalty,** Code 56.

56 **Failure to Deposit — Deposits Insufficient/Late, Taxes Paid Directly to IRS, and Incorrect Record of Federal Tax Liability** — We charged a penalty because, according to our records:

— you didn't make your tax deposit on time or in the correct amounts,
— you made one or more of your deposits to an unauthorized financial institution, paid your tax directly to the IRS or paid the tax with your return, and
— your Record of Federal Tax Liability was incomplete or illegible, or the liability amounts you reported didn't equal the net taxes for the tax period.

Form 941 series and Form 943 —If the total accumulated taxes for your return period is less than $500, you may pay this amount with your tax return.

Form 1042 — You can pay taxes of less than $200 with your tax return.

Form 720, Form 940 — You can pay taxes of $100 or less with your tax return.

Form CT-1 — You can pay taxes of less than $500 with your tax return.

If you think we should remove or reduce this penalty, see *"Removal of Penalty — Reasonable Cause."* Also see Publication 15, *Circular E — Employer's Tax Guide,* for deposit requirements.

42 **Failure To Deposit — Insufficient or Late Deposits and Taxes Paid Directly to IRS** — We charged a penalty because according to our records:

- you didn't deposit the correct amounts of tax on time, and
- you made one or more of your deposits to an unauthorized financial institution, paid your tax directly to the IRS or paid the tax with your return.

We applied your deposits and payments in the date order we received them. We used your Record of Federal Tax Liability to determine where to apply your deposits. We figured the penalty on any tax not deposited, deposited late, or not deposited in the correct amounts. For additional details see **Information on Failure to Deposit Penalty,** Code 56.

43 **Failure To Deposit — Taxes Paid Directly to IRS and Record of Federal Tax Liability Incomplete** — We charged a penalty because you paid taxes to an unauthorized financial institution, directly to the IRS, or with your tax return.

Also, your Record of Federal Tax Liability was incomplete or illegible, or the liability amounts you reported didn't equal the net taxes for the tax period. Therefore,

53 **Ten Percent Penalty for Internal Revenue Code (IRC) Section 444 Election** — We charged a penalty because we didn't receive the full amount of the "required payment" for your IRC Section 444 election on time. The required payment is the value of the tax deferral you receive when you change your tax year under IRC Section 444.

The penalty is 10% of the part of the payment that you didn't pay on time.

If the required payment is more than $500 for any year you made an IRC Section 444 election, you must make a payment with Form 8752. Required Payment or Refund Under Section 7519, by May 15th of the following calendar year. The procedures for Reasonable Cause don't apply to this 10 percent penalty.

54 **Failure to Deposit — Deposits Insufficient/Late and Incorrect Record of Federal Tax Liability** — We charged a penalty because it appears that you didn't deposit the correct amounts of tax on time. Our records showed you as a semi-weekly depositor but your Form 941, Schedule B didn't have enough information on it for us to determine if you made your deposits on time or in the correct amounts.

Therefore, we averaged the liability you reported and distributed it equally. We then applied your deposits in the date order we received them. We figured the penalty on any tax not deposited, deposited late, or not deposited in the correct amounts.

For deposits due after December 31, 1989, the penalty rate is as follows:

2% — deposits made 1 to 5 days late,
5% — deposits made 6 to 15 days late,
10% — deposits made 16 or more days late.

We figured your penalty using one of the rates listed above. **When you don't pay the amount you owe within 10 days of the date of the first notice we sent you, we automatically increase the penalty rate to 15%** and include the additional penalty in your next bill.

We averaged your total tax liability, distributed it equally, and applied your deposits and payments to the averaged liabilities in the date order we received them. We figured the penalty on any tax not deposited, deposited late, or not deposited in the correct amounts.

If you believe we computed the penalty incorrectly, please complete the enclosed Form 941, Schedule B. For additional details see **Information on Failure to Deposit Penalty** below.

Information on Failure to Deposit Penalty. There is a limit to the amount of tax you may pay with your return.

Form 941 series and Form 943 — If the total accumulated taxes for your return is less than $500, you may pay this amount with your tax return.

Form 1042 — You can pay taxes of less than $200 with your tax return.

Form 720 and Form 940 — You can pay taxes of $100 or less with your tax return.

Form CT-1 — You can pay taxes of less than $100 with your tax return.

For deposits due after December 31, 1989, the penalty rate is as follows:

2% — deposits made 1 to 5 days late,
5% — deposits made 6 to 15 days late,
10% — deposits made 16 or more days late, or
10% — deposits made to an unauthorized financial institution, or payments made directly to the IRS.

We figured your penalty using one of the rates listed above. **When you don't pay the amount you owe within 10 days of the date of the first notice we sent you, we automatically increase the penalty rate to 15%** and include the additional penalty in your next bill.

If you think we should remove or reduce this penalty, see *"Removal of Penalty — Reasonable Cause."* Also see Publication 15, Circular E — Employer's Tax Guide, for deposit requirements.

57 **Failure to Deposit — Deposits Insufficient/Late and Incorrect Record of Federal Tax Liability** — We charged a penalty because, according to our records, you didn't deposit your tax using the one-day deposit rule for liabilities $100,000 or more during a deposit period.

Also, the Record of Federal Tax Liability on your return was incomplete and we couldn't determine if you made your deposits on time or in the correct amounts. Therefore, we averaged the liability you reported and distributed it equally.

Since your average amount of monthly liability was $100,000 or more, we placed the liability on the first day of your applicable semi-weekly period. We applied your deposits in the date order we received them. We figured the penalty on any tax not deposited, deposited late, or not deposited in the correct amounts.

For deposits due after December 31, 1989, the penalty rate is as follows:

2% — deposits made 1 to 5 days late,
5% — deposits made 6 to 15 days late,
10% — deposits made 16 or more days late.

We figured your penalty using one of the rates listed above. **When you don't pay the amount you owe within 10 days of the date of the first notice we sent you, we automatically increase the penalty rate to 15%** and include the additional penalty in your next bill.

If you believe we computed the penalty incorrectly, please complete the enclosed Form 941, Schedule B. If you think we should remove or reduce this penalty, see *"Removal of Penalty — Reasonable Cause."* For information on deposit requirements, see Publication 15, *Circular E — Employer's Tax Guide*, and Publication 51, *Circular A — Agricultural Employer's Tax Guide.*

Form 941, Schedule B. If you think we should remove or reduce this penalty, see *"Removal of Penalty — Reasonable Cause."* For information on deposit requirements, see Publication 15, *Circular E — Employer's Tax Guide*, and Publication 51, *Circular A - Agricultural Employer's Tax Guide.*

Interest

09 **Interest** — We charged interest because, according to our records, you didn't pay your tax on time. We figure interest from the due date of your return (regardless of extensions) to the date we receive your full payment or the date of this notice.

Corporate Interest — We charged additional interest of 2% because, according to our records, you didn't make your corporate tax payment within 30 days after IRS notified you of the underpayment of tax. This interest begins on the 31st day after we notify you of the underpayment on tax amounts you owe over $100,000,minus your timely payments and credits.

19 **Additional Interest Charges** — Please pay the amount you owe within 10 days from the date of this notice. If we don't receive your payment by then, we will continue to charge interest until you pay your tax in full.

We will also charge a penalty for paying late. The penalty is 1/2% for each month or part of a month your tax remains unpaid from the due date of your return, but may not be more than 25% of the tax you paid late. If you think we should remove or reduce this penalty, see *": Removal of Penalty — Reasonable Cause."*

the same period of time we paid interest on the overpayment.

Status of Your Account

22 **Balance Less Than $1** — If the amount you owe is less than $1, you do not have to pay it.

23 **Refund Less Than $1** — If your refund is less than $1, we will send it to you only if you ask for it.

24 **Refund** — We will refund your overpayment (plus interest when applicable), if you owe no other taxes or have no other debts the law requires us to collect.

25 This notice is not the result of an examination of your return. We notify a taxpayer when we select his/her return for examination.

Credit Adjustments

13 **Withholding Credits** — We've made a change to your withholding tax credits.

14 **Estimated Tax Credits** — We've made a change to your estimated tax credits.

15 **Credits** — We've made a change to your credits.

29 **Erroneous Credit** — We found a credit applied to your account in error. The enclosed notice shows the correct amount due.

58 **Failure to Deposit — Deposits Insufficient/Late and Incorrect Record of Federal Tax Liability** — We charged a penalty because, according to our records, you didn't deposit your tax using the one-day deposit rule for liabilities $100,000 or more during a deposit period.

Also, your Form 941 Schedule B was incomplete and we couldn't determine if you made your deposits on time or in the correct amounts. Therefore, we averaged the liability you reported and distributed it equally.

Since your average amount of liability was $100,000 or more, we placed the liability on the first day of the applicable semi-weekly period (eighth-monthly period for tax years ending on or before December 31, 1992). We applied your deposits in the date order we received them. We figured the penalty on any tax not deposited, deposited late, or not deposited in the correct amounts.

For deposits due after December 31, 1989, the penalty rate is as follows:

2% — deposits made 1 to 5 days late,
5% — deposits made 6 to 15 days late,
10% — deposits made 16 or more days late.

We figured your penalty using one of the rates listed above. **When you don't pay the amount you owe within 10 days of the date of the first notice we sent you, we automatically increase the penalty rate to 15%** and include the additional penalty in your next bill.

If you believe we computed the penalty incorrectly, please complete the enclosed

Interest Paid

Beginning with tax year 1991, you can no longer deduct interest you paid to the Internal Revenue Service as an itemized deduction on your Form 1040, Schedule A.

Interest Reduced

If we reduce interest that you previously reported as a deduction on your tax return, you must report this reduction of interest as income on your tax return for the year we reduce it.

Interest Removed-Erroneous Refund

The law requires us to remove interest up to the date we request you to repay the erroneous refund when:

— you didn't cause the erroneous refund in any way, and
— the refund doesn't exceed $50,000.

IRS may remove or reduce interest on other erroneous refunds based on the facts and circumstances involved in each case.

Netted Interest — Effective January 1, 1987, the current interest rate we pay when you overpay your tax is 1% less than the rate of interest we charge when you underpay your tax. However, if we refund an overpayment to you with interest and we have to increase your tax at a later date, we give special consideration to the interest on these accounts.

On the tax increase after the refund, we'll charge the lower refund rate of interest on the tax instead of the higher underpayment rate of interest. We'll charge the lower interest rate on the new tax (up to the amount of the refund) for

Action Required on Balance Due Accounts

16 **Payment** — Please make your check or money order payable to the Internal Revenue Service. Write on your payment your social security number or employer identification number, the tax period and tax form. Mail your payment with the bottom part of your notice in the enclosed envelope or to the address on the front of your notice.

Notice About Partial Payments — Generally, we apply your payment first to tax, then to penalty, and finally to the interest you owe.

Additional Tax Concerns

Backup Withholding

If you received interest, dividends or patronage dividend income, but you didn't report the income on your tax return and you didn't pay the tax due on your tax return, you could be subject to a special income tax withholding called *Backup Withholding*. The IRS may request each payer of that income to begin withholding at a rate of 31 percent if, after we send you four notices over 120 days, a balance remains due on your account.

Federal/State Exchange Program

The Internal Revenue Service has agreements with state and certain local tax agencies to exchange information about federal tax, including increases or decreases. If this change affects the amount of your state or local income tax, you should file the required state or local form to report the change.

Index

I hope that the information in this book will help you with your encounters with the IRS. I also hope that you have learned more about your taxpayer's rights so that you will have more courage and confidence when you do meet with an IRS agent. Then, if you will implement some of the tax saving techniques that I have discussed, you will succeed with the objective of "How to Screw the IRS."

I welcome your comments.